In His Presence: Appreciating Your Worship Tradition

In His Presence: Appreciating Your Worship Tradition

by

ROBERT N. SCHAPER

THOMAS NELSON PUBLISHERS
Nashville • Camden • New York

Askins

Published in Nashville, Tennessee, by Thomas Nelson,
Inc., and distributed in Canada by Lawson Falle, Ltd.,
Cambridge, Ontario.

Printed in the United States of America.

Library of Congress Cataloging in Publication Data

Schaper, Robert N.
    In His presence.

    1. Public worship.   2. Liturgics.   I. Title
BV15.S33   1984   264   84-1305
ISBN 0-8407-5887-1

Contents

A Word About My Pilgrimage

I was absolutely sure that the Old Testament prophets and patriarchs looked something like him.

I wasn't supposed to be peeking, of course, but his prayer was long, and my ten-year-old mind was restless. He spoke softly, in a measured cadence, and his white moustache drooped past the corners of his mouth, giving him a sad and rather holy look. His eyes were closed, but his eyebrows were lifted high. I just knew that he was gazing into heaven.

He stood quite close to me. We were only a couple of rows from the table that stood in the center of our gathering. On it there were a loaf of bread and ten large goblets filled with grape juice.

Very shortly one of the elders would decide that the service had gone long enough, and he would step to the table and say solemnly, "Let us give thanks for the bread." We would all tear a bit from the piece that went by, and then we would wait for the goblets to be passed around. It always bothered me that the elder gave thanks for the cup, when it was so obviously *cups*.

We kids always waited to see the goblet that was passed down the row where old Peter McKnight was sitting. He thought that "drink" didn't mean "sip," so he always generously refreshed himself, and the cup emerged from his row virtually empty. I need not describe the situation on the morning when the ladies had unwittingly given us grape juice that was well on its way to becoming a vintage Concord.

As time passed, I found out that we were called "Plymouth Brethren." We didn't call our building a church because *we* were the church. There was no designated pastor, but one of the elders preached so much better than anyone else that he "pastored" most of the time.

We were very much like the Quakers, I discovered. We depended on the Spirit to guide the meeting, and you never knew exactly how it would go. You could count on some things. For instance, there would always be men who spoke, announced a hymn, or prayed. We sang *all* the stanzas of every hymn. The offering was taken in covered boxes, each with a slot in the top.

There was an abundance of preaching and Bible classes. But it was the "worship meeting" that made us unique. I didn't mind the long periods of silence when no one seemed moved to speak or sing. Sitting there and looking at that table—the fresh bread, the neatly arranged goblets, the sincere people who sat on all sides and quietly prayed or read their Bibles—I was quite sure we were in the presence of Jesus. We met every week, and it was clear that people came prepared to fellowship with Christ and with each other.

It was not until I had entered into my own pilgrimage of theological study that I began more fully to understand the significance of my worship background and how it fit into the stream of church history. For me, the pleasures of biblical, theological, and historical insight were sweet indeed. I began then what has been a lifelong search to gain a deeper understanding of the significance of worship. I felt I was gifted by the Holy Spirit to preach, but I increasingly sensed that the worship life of the church could not be satisfied by preaching alone.

My fourteen years as an evangelical pastor reinforced my deep conviction that worship must be the heartbeat of the church. I did not lessen my commitment to preaching, but I treasured ways in which the congregation could become truly involved in the worship. I especially looked forward to the celebration of the Lord's Supper.

My continued study convinced me more and more that there was another depth of meaning in the encounter with God that I and the entire church needed. I became a teacher and administrator at an evangelical school, Fuller Theological Seminary, in Pasadena, California. I was soon deeply involved in the worship life of the institution, but still I was troubled that even here there was virtually no formal study of the history and theology of worship for those potential church leaders.

I had taken courses in worship and liturgy in graduate school, and I also had begun affiliation with a church with some structure and historical tradition in its worship forms. I was exposed to more Scripture reading, creeds, prayers, and the observance of the Lord's Supper than I had previously known. I soon discovered that a disappointing sermon did not frustrate my experience of worship. The rest of the service, filled as it was with all kinds of activity on my part as a worshiper, lifted my spirit and gave me a profound awareness of the presence of Christ. At last, the pastor could have an "off" day, and the people were still able to worship!

At the seminary I was in touch with various traditions of the church. I came to recognize that there were strengths and theological values in each of them. Yet it was also evident to me that there was often a richness possible for the worshiper that either the church failed to implement or the Christian had failed to grasp. So I somewhat boldly launched full steam ahead into teaching a course on the subject of Christian worship. I read widely and practiced diligently what I taught.

In that process, I was exposed to an incredibly full range of liturgical styles. I have been in a pontifical mass in St. Peter's, and I have been in church services that included little more than an opening prayer and a sermon. I made it a point to explore, with respect and appreciation, the charismatic movement, and I discovered the re-emergence of some worship forms that the church has utilized periodically throughout its diverse history.

My pilgrimage has convinced me of the centrality of

worship in the life of the church and of the new and old possibilities for the worshiper in the traditions that are available for all of us. I am convinced that the joy of meaningful worship is not confined to any single tradition. The diversity within the body of Christ is nowhere more clear than in its worship styles.

I hope it will become apparent that the power of worship in the Christian community is not solely dependent on its form. It is humbling to discover that not everyone shares your particular taste, especially when you are convinced of the validity and beauty of your selection. As in so many aspects of our Christian life, much of what makes our worship meaningful is the mystery—the relationship of external and internal, of physical and spiritual, of outward acts and inward reality.

Whatever form we choose in worshiping, we should glorify God with the totality of our being. It seems so obvious that what we do with all our heart, soul, mind, and body has to be exciting and fulfilling. There really isn't very much in life that qualifies for that kind of participation.

I hope for all Christians what the poet Masefield called "the glory of the lighted mind." My hope for this book is that through gaining a greater understanding of the meanings behind our traditions you will thus be able to inform your own experience with a heightened sense of the grandeur and delight of true Christian worship.

1

The Primacy of Worship

When the devil met with Jesus in the wilderness, he wanted only one thing. His grandest scheme of deceit was to offer his entire treasury—all the kingdoms of this world—for one simple response from the Son of Man: "All these I will give you, if you will fall down and worship me" (Matt. 4:9).

That request, and even more the Lord's own reply, leave an unmistakable impression in our minds of the staggering, supreme significance of worship: "You shall worship the Lord your God and him only shall you serve" (Matt. 4:10). Jesus was quoting from Deuteronomy 6:13, and although we cannot be sure from that one passage just what worship really is, the ultimate significance of our relationship with God somehow seems to hang on it.

The importance of worship is further reinforced when we begin to think about the history of God's dealings with the saints of the Old Testament. Worship is the constant focus of that sacred record. It was in worship that Cain and Abel were rejected and approved. Noah worshiped God as his first act on the cleansed earth. Abraham continually set up altars to commune with God. The Mosaic Law presents the worship of God as the absolute first order of concern. "You shall have no other gods before me" and "You shall not make for yourself a graven image" (Ex. 20:3,4) are instructions for worship directed toward the nation Israel. Israel stumbled again and again over the stone of misdirected worship—idolatry. Isaiah was granted a vision of the heavenly temple and he heard a hymn being chanted by the celestial worshipers, "Holy, holy, holy is the LORD of hosts" (Is. 6:3).

Worship: Central in Christian History

This sense of the importance and significance of worship has been present in the church through its entire history. Theology—the ordering of our ideas about God—has arisen largely from the content of our worship. The defining and understanding of worship have occupied the best minds and created some of the finest literature in our history. And we all are aware that the arts, especially music, have made some of their most magnificent creative contributions to the enhancement of worship. The late theologian Karl Barth wrote, "Christian worship is the most momentous, the most urgent, the most glorious action that can take place in human life."[1]

Worship is a primary commitment in the Christian life. But our worship cannot arise from a kind of utilitarian base. We do not worship as a means to some practical end. We do not worship even to become better Christians, though we would anticipate that may well be a result. We do not worship because it will make our church better, though that too may come about. We do not worship because it will keep our family together, help other people, bring peace of mind, or assist our community. Nor do we worship because we like the choir, appreciate the preacher, or love the singing.

We worship God because He is worthy. We are Christians, and the worship of the Holy Trinity is "good, right, and our bounden duty."

If we feel, or want to feel, that kind of commitment to worship, we will then be able to transform the activities that can only serve as vehicles of true worship into the act of worship itself. Those activities or "traditions" have developed through time as a result of the desire of Christ's people to worship "in spirit and in truth" (John 4:23–24). Thus, the study of worship is not just so much history and muddling about in rather vague ideas from the past. These are appropriate words from the facade of a museum in the Palais de Chaillot in Paris: "It all depends on you whether I am a tomb or a treasure-house, whether I have much to say to you or am dumb. Do not come to me unless you are on fire to know. Yes—it all depends on you." Fortunately for us, it also depends on God.

Definition of Worship

We should not go any further without addressing the question of what we mean by worship. In some ways such a definition is amazingly complex and profound and in others it is humiliatingly simple. Worship is in that category of human experience that has a certain intuitive simplicity and philosophical complexity. It is like love. We may spend a great deal of time and mental energy defining and explaining it. And after we have gotten through, we will know what it is, though probably not as a result of the explanation. Worship is like that because it is basically the expression of a relationship. Such a relationship is always simple and complex at once, since it is a relationship between persons. It is obviously even more simple and complex when it is a relationship expressed between Creator and creature.

It should immediately be apparent that if worship is to be genuine, the relationship must be initiated and expressed by God Himself. That is not to say human beings have not attempted some initiating and expressing on their own. They have done that in great abundance, but the Judeo-Christian name for such human endeavor is idolatry. God must initiate the process, or we might well end up bowing down to sticks and stones.

Our Christian understanding of worship, then, starts with the principle that we can only come to God in worship because He has already come to us in His Son, Jesus Christ. His word to us is "Come." And He must say that word, and we must hear and obey before we can say anything at all back to Him.

As much as pastors and church leaders might like to feel it so, God is not merely inviting us to come to church as if that were an end in itself. We are to come to Him, to encounter Him. But neither do we worship the Father, Son, and Holy Spirit apart from the church. Such an encounter may, and in fact does, normally occur when the church gathers for worship. The awareness that God has made that encounter possible is what gives the corporate worship of the church the potential for excitement and meaning beyond our expectations. Yet it is the relationship, and the fact that God initiates and expresses it, that is important to us now.

If God is first, then we are second, and thus we are a necessary part of the dialogue. It must be recognized that the worship in which we engage here on earth requires the participation of us mortals. In a very real sense worship is our Spirit-led reaction to what we believe God has said and done. The grace we receive from God is ultimately invisible and internal, but it comes to us through human instruments: the Bible, the pastor, the sacraments, the music, our fellow believers. Faith appropriates what cannot be seen or proved. We believe that God has addressed us in love through Jesus Christ, and that belief prompts us to the activity of worship.

But Christian worship receives its proper dimensions when it is understood as a twofold action or encounter, a relationship in which two parties are actively involved.

God is the initiator; the Christian, or more properly Christians, are the respondents.

In English, our word *worship* roots itself in an older form that is close to "worth-ship." It means the act of ascribing worth, of expressing and demonstrating that to which we attach supreme value. It emphasizes what we do toward God. In German, one of the words for worship is *Gottesdienst*. It refers to the service of God, but as in many languages, it can also refer to the service done by someone else for God, or it can mean God's service for someone else. The second meaning is most significant. Worship means to receive from God what He pleases to do for us and to respond, not only within the moment in which He serves us, but in the entire activity of our lives.

The way in which the Bible talks about the important business of worship is instructive. The terms describing worship in the Old and New Testaments are similar. The most frequently used term in Hebrew means "to bow down," or "to prostrate oneself" (see Gen. 24:52; Ex. 4:31; 2 Chr. 7:3). The derivation or usage is not complex. There is a virtually universal response of fear, awe, or submission. We bow, kneel, or fall on our faces in the presence of greatness or majesty. In Greek, the similar term means "to kiss (the hand or the ground) toward."

The other frequently used Hebrew and Greek words are translated, "to serve." We saw that translation in the verse quoted by Jesus in the temptation, " . . . and him only shall you serve" (Matt. 4:10). In Hebrew the word relates to the straightforward idea of the servant or slave. But it is not servile or debased in the sense we might give to it. Moses and David are both called "servants of God" (see Deut. 34:5; Ps. 89:3,20). We combine those two ideas when we speak of a "worship service." Worship may lead to the service of God, but it also *is* the service of God.

Worship, therefore, we will define as *the expression of a*

relationship in which God the Father reveals Himself and His love in Christ, and by His Holy Spirit administers grace, to which we respond in faith, gratitude, and obedience. To define it, however, is not to engage in it. Our purpose in this book is to enhance and enrich our participation in that meaningful event.

Private and Corporate Worship

It would not be difficult to sense in our discussion thus far a kind of implicit assumption: worship is what happens when a group of Christians meet to adore God and respond to His grace. Simply because the adoration of God would seem to demand a grand and concerted act from His children, the assumption is true.

Yet there is an individual relationship between God and the believer, and that, too, has a proper expression, which can be called worship. Some of us may have found our personal faith to offer the most significant and rewarding experiences of our Christian life. It is amazing how many people describe their most significant encounters with God by recalling some quiet moment alone. Christians through the centuries have used various methods of directing their private times of worship toward God, and we shall look at them. It will become evident that the quality of corporate worship is always dependent on the private devotion of those who gather—and vice versa.

In fact, the reverse is more true than most of us have imagined. The church at worship is the gathered church. What kind of understanding we have of God, the Bible, prayer, and many other basic Christian realities will be learned primarily in the gathered community of faith. The whole orientation of the New Testament is toward ministry to a gathered church. The gifts of the Spirit are for the purpose of building up, or edifying, the people of God. That is obviously not on just a one-to-one basis. The very writing of the New Testament literature assumes a gathered church that will receive the word joyfully and obediently.

To see this in the Epistles is easy. Paul and the others wrote letters to the churches, and they even gave instructions for the sharing of those letters between congregations (see Col. 4:16). It is certainly plausible that the preaching of the apostles was based on their retelling of the stories and teachings found in our Gospels. The occasion for such preaching and rehearsing of the events of the life of Jesus was the gathering of those Christians from week to week in order to worship.

Our purpose in discussing worship is to understand and enrich the expression of a relationship that is both individual and corporate. Because we are part of the body of Christ, corporate worship will express the relationship best. Because we are members in particular, private worship will also be necessary and meaningful (see 1 Cor. 12:27).

Plan for This Study

How do we go about this study? The only place to begin is with the Bible itself, and we will take a good look at the worship of the people of God in Old Testament times. That will lead historically to the important development of the synagogue, with some reference to contemporary Jewish worship. Then we will survey the New Testament material on worship. The first four centuries were extremely important for the church and its worship practices, so we will take a careful look at the developments of that formative period.

Then we will look at the movement from the Orthodox church, through the Middle Ages, and on to the present. We will look carefully at the Roman Catholic church and its mass. That will include the amazing changes of the Second Vatican Council, with the hope it will open our understanding of what kinds of things make up Roman Catholic worship today.

This will be followed by a look at the major traditions that stem from the Reformation and later. We will group together, yet view individually, the Lutherans and Episcopalians, the Presbyterians and Methodists, the Baptists, Congregationalists, Churches of Christ, and Independents, and then the Quakers, Pentecostals, and neo-Pentecostals. Remember, this is not just "history." It is the important and interesting story of your fellow church members and their heritage.

Following our examination of the various traditions, we will look at the question of sacraments and symbolism, a most important part of our understanding of the motives for worship. Then we shall try to describe worship as a way of life, looking at the attitudes that shape our approach to it and the possibilities for our participation. We will expand on this by seeing how our entire Christian life is reflected and experienced in our worship.

Since we worship both privately and corporately, we will explore the devotional practices of Christians as individuals with an eye to the enrichment of this aspect of our service to God. We will close with a survey of problems and prospects. There are difficulties in worship today, and we need to explore ways to meet them and directions the Holy Spirit seems to be indicating for our future.

Above all, we are moving toward a renewed, enlivened, meaningful life in the worship of God, both in our private moments and in our times of gathering with God's people to bring glory and honor to the God whom heaven and earth adore.

The following questions and discussion topics are designed to make each chapter contribute most creatively to your understanding and appreciation of worship. They are also intended to push your thinking beyond the contents of the chapter.

Group discussion depends on a variety of factors. Some questions will be more helpful and provocative than others. The studious reader is urged to read the Scripture verses cited. Those will also be useful in any group study.

It is only natural that the "case studies" for this book will arise from the available experiences and traditions of the reader or the church group. Use your own worship service as a basis of reflection, and draw in other denominational leaders as possible.

1. Discuss the sources of feelings and attitudes you associate most readily with worship.
2. What have been your most significant worship experiences?
3. Worship is defined as the "expression of a relationship." Why must we think first about God's part in it?
4. Is there a good reason to define worship as the expression of a relationship rather than just as a relationship? Why?
5. What do you feel is most deficient about corporate worship as you experience it?
6. What contribution does private devotion make to corporate worship?
7. Can you relate the "response in faith, gratitude, and obedience" to the various parts of corporate worship?

8. Is it right to observe that "God does not invite us to come to church"? Isn't that dangerous?
9. What do you anticipate from a study of worship?

[1]Quoted in J. J. von Allmen, *Worship: Its Theology and Practice* (London: Lutterworth, 1965) p. 13.

2

Worship in the Old Testament

How did God's people worship during Old Testament times? The Old Testament, remember, covers a period significantly longer than the Christian era. Just as a worshiper of the fourth century A.D. might approach his task quite differently from the way we do today, so there were various stages and processes at work in the history of the worship of Israel.

It is also true that some of the material we have in the Old Testament can be rather obscure regarding the actual worship practice of a particular time. Some accounts come in the form of vignettes, almost like flash pictures, with very little background filled in. There are some interesting examples. First Samuel 9:22 describes a meal derived from sacrifices, the guests being invited by Samuel. About thirty were served by "the cook" and it all seems to be part of a worship ritual. Samuel also led a ceremony (see 1 Sam. 7:6) of pouring water out on the ground before the Lord. Isaiah 30:29 speaks of a worship procession, possibly at night, accompanied by the playing of a flute. There are numbers of holy processions mentioned in the Psalms (see 26:6; 42:4; 68:25), and those included some kind of ritual dancing (see Ps. 87:7; 149:3; 150:4). The story is famous of David's dance before the Lord, which was not appreciated by his wife (see 2 Sam. 6:14).

All this is to say that there were ceremonies and rituals that formed a meaningful part of worship in Israel that we do not fully understand. Some seem vestiges of much earlier, primitive rites. But some very significant practices do emerge that we Christians should take seriously. As with the New Testament, the Old Testament abounds with glorious imagery as to sacred places, times, and actions.

Sacred Places

1. The Temple

Very early the worship of God was associated with specific places. God appeared to the ancients in various manifestations, and the locale involved became significant. A tree, a spring, a stone, or pile of stones would mark a spot of divine encounter to which people evidently returned to pray or offer sacrifice. Later, although those various shrines continued to exist throughout Israel, the worship became more and more centered in Jerusalem.

Central to Israel's form of worship was the experience of the Exodus. During that forty years in transit the people were united both by their experiences and by the giving of the Covenant. Then, after the people entered the promised land, the culture and the religious unity were lost during the period of the Judges, but were regained under the rulership of David and with the building of Solomon's Temple.

That holy place was filled with the sacred memories of Abraham, the Exodus, and David. Abraham had offered Isaac to God with the subsequent divine intervention and provision (see Gen. 22:9-14). David had purchased a threshing floor and made a sacrifice (see 1 Chr. 21:18-27). With the divinely given specifications for the tabernacle of the Exodus now resident in the Temple building and its furniture, the worship of God was more and more assumed to be appropriate only at or facing toward that holy site. Since it was the one place that eventually was authorized as the place of sacrifice, no Jewish worship was really complete without it.

There is one factor regarding the Temple as a sacred site that we should particularly notice. Although the Israelites often called it the dwelling place of God, this place was primarily regarded as a place of meeting with God rather than as His actual dwelling. We will remember that the Ark of the Covenant was the great unoccupied throne, and the tabernacle was called "the tent of meeting." It was the place of encounter with God, but not because God was *only* there. The Hebrew concept of God was far too large, too transcendent to tolerate such a view. It was the dwelling place of God, which made God fully and graciously accessible. But God was above all and beyond all, and the Jews never doubted that.

2. The Home

We will also do well to notice the way in which the home became a kind of holy place in Jewish thinking and practice. The patriarchal roots of Jewish religion brought a special sanctification to the place where the family lived. In a way that could prove instructive to the Christian community, Judaism made the home an annex of the Temple and created under divine guidance many events for the home and family that were shared by all and were vital to the worship of the community.

Genesis 17 gives us the story of circumcision, given by God to Abraham as a sign of God's covenant with him and his descendants (see Gen. 17:10). The language is so direct that circumcision seems to be the covenant itself, rather than a sign of it. That is an early demonstration of what we will study later in the church as sign and sacrament. The spiritual nature of this rite is clearly preserved in such passages as Deuteronomy 10:16 and Jeremiah 4:4 and 9:25. In the latter passage, the prophet referred to the disobedient Israelites as "uncircumcised in heart." That principle was repeated by John the Baptist (see Luke 3:8), by Jesus, and by Paul (see Rom. 2:25). Our point, however, is that that important event, a sacred rite for the Jews, was performed in the home with family and neighbors as the joyful participants.

Though not an event that would normally be considered as worship, religious instruction was to be given at home (see Gen. 18:19; Ex. 13:8; Ps. 78:3-6). This was finally taken over in part by the synagogue, but as we shall see in the discussion of Passover, the responsibility of making clear the content of the faith of Israel was in the home.

One of the recurring events that would assist in this and also create an act of worship in the home was the Sabbath observance, which included the Sabbath blessing. One may add to this the blessings before and after meals. It must be noted that the home was not a sacred place in the sense of sharing the same religious significance as the Temple or the other shrines. However, the home participated as a locale for worship events. This will help explain how the synagogue as an alternative sacred place could come into being in Jewish theology.

Sacred Time—The Sabbath

With the presence of the Sabbath, we move into a discussion of the *sanctifying of time*, a practice not uniquely the possession of Israel, but significantly developed by her.

That time can be sanctified—set apart for God from common use—is an amazing phenomenon. Our interest is to see clearly that the making of a holy day was an act of devotion that was uniquely "for the Lord." The day was not for the purpose of a feast. There was no sacrifice specified. The worshiper did not go anywhere. In fact, he was carefully regulated so that he would not journey.

The underlying reality was to be that the Israelites would give back to God one day in each seven. The day was to be kept free from dissipation of attention, interest, or energy for any purpose other than worship. To consecrate that one span of time was to acknowledge God's rightful claim to all of the people's time.

There might have been certain agricultural or psychological influences that would make the Hebrews responsive to one day of rest in seven. The theological base for it is rooted in the Decalogue, which reminded the people that God rested the seventh day and that their rest properly imitated His. But that means of making the day holy, by stopping normal activities so that the time was God's, was a unique and profound step in the understanding of worship.

It is difficult for the modern Christian community to understand the consecration of time. We are very much caught up in the significance of actions. It must be admitted that the Hebrew theologians, too, finally buried the spiritual significance of the Sabbath as sacred time in the avalanche of legalism regarding what could and could not be done on the Sabbath (see Mark 2:23–28). To read the elaborate schemes the rabbis developed in the oral law, now preserved for us in the Talmud, is overwhelming. Jesus and the apostles rightly reacted against this.

But to keep the Sabbath for man rather than vice versa is not to destroy its meaning. There is no reason that the idea of the consecration of time cannot be preserved for us in the Lord's Day of the Christian community, but it may take some doing. The move from holy days to holidays marked by recreation and amusement is problem enough. But the deeper significance of time itself as belonging to God, and thereby influencing our ideas of what we do with that time, easily avoids us.

Sacred Actions or Events

Having looked briefly at places and times for worship in Israel, we now will consider the rituals and ceremonies that were used. But first we should define some terms.

Liturgy is from two Greek words and it means "the work of the people." But it is for us a theological word that refers to the structure or events of a particular service of corporate worship. In one sense every service of worship has a liturgy, an agreed-upon procedure, so that people are not doing a number of different things all at once. The liturgy of a particular Old Testament sacrifice would be a description of what the priest did and said and what the worshiper was instructed to do.

Another word used in the study of worship is *cult*. This is taken from the Latin word *cultus*, which simply means "worship." Until the eighteenth century, cult merely meant the worship practices of some particular group or religion. Since then it often has been applied to the group itself, especially to adherents of some heretical or bizarre group that departs from orthodox belief. In our study, we will use the word *cult* to refer to the corporate worship of a particular body.

The cult of the Temple, then, would be the various worship activities carried on there. The liturgy would be the activity for a specific feast or sacrifice. We will now examine those two actions, feast and sacrifice.

Feasts

By the time of Christ, there were seven annual Jewish festivals: Passover, Pentecost, Tabernacles, Atonement, New Year, Purim, and Lights. The first three were pilgrimage festivals, and it was expected that as many as could would go to Jerusalem for the observance (see Ex. 23:17; Deut. 16:16–17).

In the process of time those feasts were connected with

three great historical events at the beginning of Israel's history—Passover with the Exodus, Pentecost with the giving of the Law at Sinai, and Tabernacles with the wilderness wanderings. The Christian community, of course, has given special attention to Passover because of its connection with the Lord's Supper and the Crucifixion. St. Paul speaks of "Christ our Passover" (see 1 Cor. 5:7).

Let us note briefly and systematically what the seven feasts celebrated.

1. *Passover* (also Unleavened Bread—see Ex. 12; Lev. 23:4-5; Deut. 16:1-8). This meal was first eaten at home. It was probably with the recovery of the Book of Deuteronomy in the time of Josiah that it became a national feast, the lambs being killed at the Temple. The feast was in remembrance of the slaying of the firstborn of Egypt and of God's deliverance of Israel. We will take a closer look at this very joyous, domestic festival later. It lasted seven days.

2. *Pentecost* (see Lev. 23:9-21). The name is from the Greek word for fifty, since fifty days were measured from the beginning of Passover to this feast. The Jews called it the Feast of Weeks or the Feast of Harvest. It marked the completion of the barley harvest and was a time of great national rejoicing and festivity.

3. *Tabernacles* (see Lev. 23:33-43). This was also called the Feast of Booths, since everyone was supposed to construct some type of temporary shelter, a tent or lean-to, and live in it during the festival of seven days. Why was a "booth" significant? This was a vivid remembrance of the wilderness trek, but originally it was a festival for the fall harvest.

4. *Feast of Trumpets* (later *Rosh Hashanah* or "New Year"—see Lev. 23:24-25; Num. 29:1-6). A solemn convocation to mark the beginning of a religious year, not the calendar year, New Year was on the first of the seventh

month. One of its marks was the blowing of the *shofar*, the ceremonial trumpet.

5. *Atonement* (*Yom Kippur*—see Lev. 16:1–34). This high, holy day was a day of fasting that came at the end of the ten penitential days begun with New Year. The high priest offered sacrifice for himself, the Temple, and the people. In the calendar of modern Israel the observance begins with the famous *Kol Nidre* ("all vows") which is a repentance for broken vows during the previous year.

6. *Purim* (see Esth. 9). The name is from the Assyrian word *puree*, written *pur* in our Bible (see Esth. 3:7). It means "lot," or "pebble," and probably refers to the casting of a lot. The feast celebrates the deliverance of the Jews from Haman. It is not mentioned in the New Testament.

7. *Lights* (also called Feast of Dedication). This commemorated the cleansing of the Temple by Judas Maccabeus in 164 B.C. This is known in modern times by the term *Hanukah*, which means "consecration." It has become the Jewish winter festival roughly corresponding to the Christmas season.

The point for us in this catalog of festivals is to see how God ordered Jewish worship so that, at regular intervals during the year, there were exciting celebrations of God's great works of deliverance and salvation. The festivals were elaborate, they were demanding, they were joyous for the most part, and they were interesting.

A good illustration of this is the observance of the Seder or Passover. Many Christians are paying more and more attention to that observance as a kind of bridge between Judaism and Christianity. The liturgy is fascinating.

A *Kiddush*, or sanctifying prayer, begins the service. There are four cups of wine, which are drunk at different times. The unleavened bread is called mazzah, or mazzoth, and is known to non-Jews as matzo. There are four passages in the Torah (Pentateuch, or Books of Moses) that tell the Jews what they are to say "when your children say to you, 'What do you mean by this service?'" (Ex. 12:26–27 NKJV; see also 13:8–9; 13:14–15; Deut. 6:20–25).

The Jews assigned those four questions to four sons, and they are clever and instructive to say the least. The first son is wise and asks the question sincerely. The second son is hostile and is reproved. The third son is genuinely ignorant of the meaning, and the fourth is made out to be disorganized and foolish. All four questions about the ceremony are followed by an explanation called, in Hebrew, the *Haggadah*, a lengthy rehearsal by the father of all that God has done for Israel since Abraham. Jews of more recent times follow this part of the ceremony by singing a lively song from the sixth century A.D.

Then follows the recitation of two psalms from the *Hallel* ("Praise," the first part of *Hallelujah*), Psalms 113 and 114. A blessing, the washing of hands, and eating is followed by another long blessing, then the remainder of the *Hallel*, Psalms 115—118 and Psalm 136. The modern liturgy has concluded with the phrase, "Next year in Jerusalem."

This is a home service, and the traditions have been built around children and the family. The children hide a piece of unleavened bread and demand a ransom for bringing it back. There is a lot of singing, and the songs are fun as well as being religious history. The "Madrigal of Numbers" (very like the "Twelve Days of Christmas") starts with the thirteen attributes of God and works down: twelve tribes, eleven stars, ten commandments, nine months of carrying, eight days of the Covenant, seven days in the week, six orders of the *Mishnah* (Talmud), five books of the Law, four mothers (just who is not certain), three fathers (Abraham, Isaac, and Jacob), two tables of the Covenant, and one God.

It is apparent that the Passover, like the other festivals,

served to unleash the finest and most fervent feelings of love, relationship, community, and above all, gratitude to God for His mighty acts on their behalf.

Sacrifices

There were other sacred events in the worship life of Israel besides the feasts. Far more frequent, and filled with meaning all their own, were the sacrifices. Sacrifice has been a part of worship from the very beginning. Basically it is life offered to God, but it has other implications.

For the Jews there were at least four meanings or uses for sacrifice. One was *expiation*, that is, the cleansing of sin by the giving of life in place of and on behalf of the worshiper. A second use of sacrifice was for *food*. There was a divine restraint placed on the Hebrews. They never suggested that the food was for God. It was for the priests and in some instances for the worshiper. When given solely for God, it was burned up. The use as food for priest and worshiper also involved the third meaning of sacrifice: *fellowship*. This was a kind of eating before God rather than eating with Him (see Deut. 12:7). A fourth meaning in sacrifice was that of *gift*. There were various "sacrifices" that did not involve slaughter, but were the presentation of different items as expressions of thankfulness to God, a gift to God who had given first.

There were basically three classes of sacrifices for the Hebrews: (1) the burnt offering was for God and all of it was consumed by the fire (see Lev. 1:1–17; 6:8–13); (2) offerings for sin and guilt were partly burned and partly consumed by the priests (see Lev. 4:1—6:7; 6:24—7:10); and (3) peace offerings (see Lev. 3:1–17; 7:11–34) were a shared meal with the priests.

The description of the sacrifices in the Old Testament is sketchy at best. We know that there was a morning and evening sacrifice daily in the Temple. Those could be very grand occasions. In one of the books of the Apocrypha, a collection of religious writings from the time between the Old and New Testament periods, the writer described an occasion of festival sacrifice from the time of a high priest "Simon, the son of Onias." This is part of the description in Ecclesiasticus 50:11–20 (NEB):

> When he put on his gorgeous vestments,
> robed himself in perfect splendour,
> and went up to the holy altar,
> he added lustre to the court of the sanctuary.
> When the priests were handing him the portions of the sacrifice,
> as he stood by the altar hearth
> with his brothers round him like a garland,
> he was like a young cedar of Lebanon
> in the midst of a circle of palms....
> he held out his hand for the libation cup
> and poured out the blood of the grape,
> poured its fragrance at the foot of the altar
> to the Most High, the King of all.
> Then the sons of Aaron shouted
> and blew their trumpets of beaten silver;
> they sounded a mighty fanfare
> as a reminder before the Lord.
> Instantly the people as one man fell on their faces
> to worship the Lord their God, the Almighty, the Most High.
> Then the choir broke into praise,
> in the full sweet strains of resounding song....
> Then Simon came down and raised his hands
> over the whole congregation of Israel,
> to pronounce the Lord's blessing,
> proud to take his name on his lips.

This is obviously a festal celebration in a grand style.

There might be an impression from this description that

the forgiveness of sins would come to the worshiping Israelite as a matter of course. Sacrifice offered—sins forgiven. There is abundant evidence that this wasn't the case, at least not in the theology of Israel's leadership. No words could be more direct than Proverbs 15:8: "The sacrifice of the wicked is an abomination to the LORD." True penitence was asked and expected. That all did not give it was as true then as today.

But that still leaves us with some ambiguity about what the worshiper, the "layman" of Israel, was supposed to do. We do know that worship had become centralized and formalized under the direction of the priests in Jerusalem. More and more the liturgy was removed from the people. When a person was involved in a ceremony he did only a few things: he said amen to prayers and rites; he said or shouted hallelujah as part of the worship; he laid his hands on the sacrifice to show his identity with it; he was expected to observe the Sabbath, revere the Torah, show kindness and justice in dealing with neighbors, and love and obey God with all his heart, mind, soul, and strength. After all, each person was a member of the people of God—the congregation—at all times, and every part of life was affected by that covenant relationship.

Psalms

One source that we might overlook in an exploration of worship is the great collection of hymns known as the Psalms. Here is an amazing prayer book that reflects the religious life of David and numbers of other authors. The psalms arose both from private and public devotion and are comprehensive in their scope. The range of content is awesome:

1. *The Creation*. The wonders of God's world are a constant source of inspiration (see Ps. 8; 19). This includes the

storms (Ps. 29) and rain (Ps. 65:9ff), which was so important to the agricultural cycle of Palestine.

2. *History*. This was the second great focus of the psalmists. Nature and history correspond to creation and redemption. To the Hebrew, the revelation of God was history (see Ps. 105; 136). This included the culmination of history with the reign of God (see Ps. 47; 96).

3. *Worship*. It is difficult to know exactly which Psalms may have been used in temple worship, but some certainly were (e.g., see Ps. 42; 43; 48; 84).

4. *Human Experience*. These range far—penitence, joy, fear, revenge, despair, exultation. There is no human emotion or condition that is not mirrored in many places (see Ps. 6; 32; 38; 51; 102; 130).

The Psalms are varied and wide-ranging not only in content but also in type. There are many ways to classify the Psalms, but one way is to divide them according to whether they are personal and private or national and corporate. They further divide into praise and thanksgiving or penitence and lament.

The church has virtually always used the Psalms in liturgy in spite of the personal nature of many of them. The "I" and other personal pronouns become proper reminders that corporate worship is always the result of the combined action of individuals. There is no "we" without an "I." We have even used the Psalms in worship in spite of the fact that a given psalm may not express the feelings of an entire congregation. To be aware that someone does feel a certain way and needs to express it is a gracious acceptance of our responsibility to each other in the body of Christ.

Basic Elements of Worship

What are the basic elements of Old Testament worship that emerge from our overview? Specific liturgies may not be available, but the major principles are present. The Psalms give us the best tests to show this.

1. *Adoration*. This includes reverence and awe, demonstrated both in posture and word (see Ps. 95:6; 99:5; 8:1; 22:3; 33:8). One thinks especially of Moses at the burning bush (see Ex. 3:5). Adoration is considered the proper obligation of the worshiper, and it is to be done for no other reason than it is right to do it and therefore our duty (see Ps. 96:7-9).

2. *Praise and thanksgiving*. This is the declaration of grateful thanks for God's mighty acts and the blessings they bring (see Ps. 5:7; 34:1-3; 107:1; 145:21). The praise of God was expressed by the Hebrews with the word *bless*. God's blessings are abundant and gracious, and the proper response is to give our energy, our thoughts, and our thanks and glory back to God. We "bless" the Lord (because He has blessed us) in that we give praise and thanks to Him (Ps. 103:1). This praise includes singing and the playing of musical instruments (see Ps. 27:6; 89:1; 92:1-4; 105:1-6). The music of the Israelites must have been loud and piercing, even though it is described often as sweet and beautiful. One of the Hebrew words used to describe the singing of worshipers also referred to the battle cry! At least the singing was vigorous! Some of the singing was certainly antiphonal.

3. *Confession and penitence*. This is an Old Testament principle, but it is not very clearly present as a liturgical action. It seems to have had a liturgical setting. The famous cry, "O Lord, open thou my lips; and my mouth shall show forth thy praise" (Ps. 51:15), seems to imply a congregational kind of response. Psalm 32 is a similar case, and to the extent that the Psalms were indeed written with a worship context in mind, that is an evidence of a formal and public kind of confession and repentance (see also Ps. 6, 38, 102, 130, and 143). Isaiah 6:5 shows penitence to be the proper response to the vision of God.

4. *Prayer of petition*. This is put in a personal mode in the Psalms (see 27:12; 31:4; 35:17–18; 64:1–2; 69:1ff; 116:3ff; 118:25). There are many such prayers scattered through the Old Testament, but not many in a setting of corporate worship.

5. *Prayer of intercession*. There is very little to go on in the way of intercession as part of the worship. The Psalms confine it to prayers for the king (see Ps. 20) and general concerns for Israel and Jerusalem. Outside the Psalter there are many occasions of intercession, but not necessarily in a worship context. Abraham, Moses, and Samuel interceded for Israel (see Gen. 18:23; Ex. 32:31ff; 1 Sam. 12:23). Solomon publicly interceded for the people in the great prayer of dedication for the Temple (1 Kin. 8:23ff). One has to add to this the intercessory work of the priest on behalf of the worshiper and all the people.

We should not leave the subject of Old Testament worship without these final thoughts. There is a kind of running battle in the Old Testament between the priestly work centered in the Temple and that of the prophet who appeared regularly to thunder against corrupt practices by priest, king, and people. Though some have attempted to suggest it, there is no evidence that the formal, structured worship of the Temple was a development unauthorized by God. The prophet detected the hypocrisy of a worship that could continue externally and be lifeless internally. That possibility exists in any corporate structure.

The repeated failure brought about by our human frailty is nowhere more evident than in the history of worship. We seem determined to substitute something else in the place of heartfelt and sincere adoration of God. Perhaps our pride and hypocrisy more easily produce formalism than anything else, but Israel's history and ours show that genuine worship is never simply the result of finding the right format.

Although the feasts and sacrifices of the ancient Hebrews are far removed from us in time and culture, many of the basic attitudes and responses of our worship are deeply imbedded in the Old Testament and in Jewish practice. Above all, we can see in their practices a desire to offer all to God—both the joyfulness of praise and thanksgiving and the anguish of sin and sorrow.

The many prayers and conversations recorded in the Old Testament reveal a deep awareness of the dialogue between God and His people, and from those pages we can learn much that will enrich our own worship. We shall discuss the themes of offering and worship as dialogue in a later chapter. At this point it will be helpful to see how the Old Testament practices carried on in the worship of the synagogue.

STUDY GUIDE

1. What have you imagined the worship experiences of an Israelite to have been, say, in the time of Samuel, or Solomon?
2. Can you suggest both good and bad results from the building of the Temple?
3. What do you consider applicable to the Christian home from the practices of ancient Judaism? Can there be in our contemporary world something of worship in the home?
4. The "Lord's Day" is not a mere duplication of the Sabbath. Without getting too involved, suggest how the Lord's Day has changed or preserved the Sabbath practices and evaluate. (Read Ex. 20:8–11; 31:12–17; Num. 15:32–36; Jer. 17:19–23; Ezek. 20:12; Mark 2:23–28.)

5. What is in your mind when you say a church is "liturgical"?

6. As you review the activities of the Jewish feasts, what experiences do you see that are never in essence duplicated in your experience as a worshiper? (Read Ex. 12; Lev. 16 and 23; Deut. 16:1–8.)

7. How did the Jews preserve the inner and spiritual in the routine of their worship?

8. Read together a psalm from each of the groups listed.

9. Why do you think the ancient church read a psalm *after* reading a Scripture lesson rather than reading a psalm *as* a lesson?

10. Can you apply the "battle" between priest and prophet to the church today?

3

Worship in the Synagogue

In 200 B.C., a rabbi named Simon the Just said that the world rested on three pillars; namely, the Torah, Worship, and the Bestowal of Kindnesses. Perhaps those pillars summarize Jewish religious life—instruction in the way of God, the humble adoration of God, and wisdom in the daily affairs of life. It was the premium placed on instruction and worship that brought the synagogue into existence.

Development

The attempt of the Temple to keep its activity central to the religious life of Israel had many natural hindrances. Three festivals were required, but they offered, at best, a marginal involvement for most of the people. The authorities instituted a group of lay representatives to be present at the daily services. A *ma'amad* was a group of men from some outlying district, which roughly corresponded to the twenty-four courses of levitical priests who came to serve at the Temple two separate weeks of each year. While some members of the *ma'amad* were at Jerusalem, the other members would meet in their own town for prayer at times fixed to correspond with the sacrifices. This was designed to keep a focus on Jerusalem, but it did gather pious men for the worship of God in their own community.

The Temple further suffered as the Law became more prominent. To be sure, there were cultic demands for central worship. But holiness of life would increasingly be measured by ethical and moral rather than cultic standards. The respected authorities were those who knew the Law, not those who performed the sacrifices.

The turning point came with the Babylonian captivity and the destruction of the Temple (sixth century B.C.). The people were now in a foreign land. How could Yahweh be with them, and how could they hope to worship without a Temple and sacrifice (see Ps. 137)? Ezekiel consoled and assured them:

> Thus says the Lord GOD: Though I removed them far off among the nations, and though I scattered them among the countries, yet I have been a sanctuary to them for a while [or, in small measure] in the countries where they have gone (Ezek. 11:16).

It was an absolute necessity that they somehow meet together and preserve their traditions. They no longer were living in an environment where everything reminded them that they were a covenant people. They no longer were under leaders who fostered the observance of the Torah. The few who managed to return to Israel found a difficult situation in which to revive their traditions, and the many who remained scattered struggled to preserve the heritage of hundreds of years of history.

Purpose

Such a challenge always demands a sharpened focus of religious purpose. What was the tradition to be preserved? It proved to be twofold. The first was instruction. That is the basic meaning of the word *Torah*. For instruction to take place, there had to be a gathering of the people to read and study the Torah. The community needed to know what God wanted them to do, and that had been graciously revealed in the Torah.

To receive such instruction was to be called to prayer, and that was the second purpose of the synagogue. It was a place of devotion. There could be no sacrifice outside the Temple, but there could be prayer. Gradually a set of traditions emerged as to what the worshiping community would do when it gathered for devotional purposes.

There is an importance to this order. The priorities of any community will profoundly affect the way it worships. When we move into the synagogue we are moving much closer to Jesus and the early church. It is interesting to note that Jesus taught both in the Temple and in the synagogue. Of the Temple He said, "My house shall be a house of prayer."

Function

What was done in the synagogue at the beginning of the Christian era, and what is done today? Both of those questions should interest the Christian worshiper.

The early synagogues were of simple construction as far as floor plan was concerned, although they could be elegant buildings, depending on the given situation. There was at least one synagogue in each city of moderate to large size in Palestine at the time of Christ. The amazing vitality of the institution was shown by the fact that there were said to be 394 in Jerusalem itself, right in the shadow of the Temple!

There were detailed specifications for the building of synagogues. The site was always supposed to be the highest place in the city, although that regulation was often violated if land elsewhere was available. In the synagogue was a raised platform at one end, called the *bema*. On it there was an ark, a decorated receptacle for the scrolls of the

Law and the Prophets. There were a lectern for the readings, seats for the elders, and a special seat for the leader. There was an attendant who cared for the cleaning and lighting, brought the Scriptures to the reader, and also inflicted punishment on unruly students or those who were disciplined. The ruler or president was responsible for the conduct of worship and maintenance of order. Ten men were necessary to form a synagogue. Those various personnel are mentioned in the New Testament (see Luke 4:20; 8:41; 13:14; Matt. 10:17; 23:24).

The service was fairly simple. It began with introductory prayers and psalms that preceded the great confession of Israel, the *Shema*. The first prayer was the *Yotzer*, a prayer of thanks for creation, and the second was called *Ahabah*, the word for love. Those were *berakoth*, blessings that began with the oft-used phrase, *Baruk attah Adonai* ("Blessed art Thou, O Lord").

Then the *Shema* was recited: "Hear, O Israel: the LORD our God, the LORD is one! ..." (Deut. 6:4 NKJV). Several Scripture verses are included with that great affirmation, including Deuteronomy 6:4–9, 11:13–21, and Numbers 15:37–41. Another benediction followed, called the *Geullah*, which speaks of God as Redeemer. In the evening there was a fourth benediction, called *Hashkibenu*, "Cause us to lie down."

Then followed the prayers. They are known as the *Amidah*, which means "standing." If there were not ten people present, the prayers were silent. There eventually came to be a collection of prayers known as the *Shemoneh Esreh*, which simply means "eighteen." Actually there were finally nineteen, but no one bothered to change the title! Certain subjects and suggestions for prayer undoubtedly arose quite early in the history of the synagogue, and then various items were added. One of those, the twelfth prayer, was inserted at some point after the beginnings of Christianity. It is attributed to a rabbi named Samuel the Small, around the year A.D. 100. That benediction is called *Buikath-ha-Minim*. The "Minim" are heretics, and the prayer seems to refer to Christians as well:

> For apostates let there be no hope, and the dominion of ar-rogance do thou speedily root out in our days: and let the "Notzerim" [Christians?] and heretics perish as in a mo-ment, let them be blotted out of the book of the living and let them not be written with the righteous. Blessed art thou, O Lord, who humblest the arrogant.

That prayer is from the text of the *Palestinian Amidah* and such a prayer is not repeated in the present-day Jewish prayer book. *Notzerim* is probably a variation of "Naza-renes." It would obviously be an impossibility for any Jew-ish Christian to recite that prayer in the synagogue.

If an Aaronic priest was present, he was privileged to give the Aaronic benediction (see Num. 6:22-26) between the sixth and seventh prayers of the *Amidah*: "The LORD bless thee, and keep thee: the LORD make his face shine upon thee, and be gracious unto thee: the LORD lift up his countenance upon thee, and give thee peace" (vv. 24-26 KJV).

One church father reported that for that priestly blessing the congregation stood with their hands raised as high as their shoulders, repeating the formula word by word after the priest and responding with *Amen* after each of the three parts of the blessing. The use of the *Amen* by the wor-shipers was quite ancient (see Ps. 41:13; 72:19; 89:52; 106:48), and the practice was quickly adopted by the New Testament church, as we shall see.

The Reading of Scripture came next. That reading was done three days each week. The major service was, of course, on the Sabbath, but there were readings in the synagogue on the second and fifth days of the week also. The only indication of a reason for selecting those days was that in many places they were market days, and a larger number of people would be gathered in the village or town.

On the Sabbath there were seven readers, if possible, and on other days there were three. Prayers were said and the *Shema* was recited three times each day, but the Torah was read only twice on the Sabbath and twice during the week. By the first century A.D. it had been divided into 150 sections so that it could be read through once in three years.

The Prophets were read on the Sabbath only. That reading is known as the *Haphtarah*. Not only was the Scripture read, it was translated, since in later times the people did not understand Hebrew. The translation into Aramaic was called the Targum, and very specific traditions grew up surrounding it. Then followed the sermon, called the Midrash, which was an exposition of Scripture, though not necessarily the passage that had been read. The preacher sat, as did the people. They stood to pray and recite the *Shema*.

Women in the Synagogue

There is no avoiding the fact there was patriarchal domination of worship life in Judaism, even in the synagogue. One of the daily prayers was a thanksgiving "that I am not a woman" (from the Babylonian Talmud, "Menahoth," 43b). There have been clever interpretations to reduce the stark character of this statement. It is pointed out that the man was expressing gratitude that more of the Torah was incumbent on him, since women were exempted from some obligations. It is also suggested that this was a simple self-affirmation and that a woman could therefore properly thank God she was not a man, since God did not make her such.

But when all is said, it is still the fact that women were generally subordinated and regarded with condescension or suspicion. However, the segregation of women in worship, or their exclusion from it is not at all proven by the record, at least in the first century. They were not counted as members of the synagogue, but some sources indicate they were permitted to take part in the reading. They were zealous in their attendance, and there is no clear evidence of their being segregated in the service until the fourth century in Babylon. Paul's experience of the conversion of various women who were synagogue participants demonstrates that women both attended and gave careful attention (see Acts 16:14).

The Synagogue and the Church

There can be no question that the worship of the synagogue had a profound influence on the worship of the church, though perhaps it was more in the subject and general framework of worship than in matters of specific content.

There is no evidence, for instance, that the *Shema* ("Hear, O Israel") or *Amidah* (eighteen prayers) were ever used in the early church. There are some strong historical reasons for this. The *Shema* was forbidden to the Jews, and presumably the Christians, by Hadrian at the time of the Jewish uprising under Bar-cochba around the year A.D. 135. The Jews responded by "hiding" it in their third benediction, the *Kedushah*, which read: "Holy art thou, and thy Name is to be feared, and there is no God beside Thee. Blessed art thou, O Lord, the Holy God." But it does appear that even if the Christians had used it before, once they dropped it there was no reason to use it again.

There is also an interesting bit of history in the Christian use of the Decalogue, the Ten Commandments, as part of their service. In pre-Christian times the Jews had recited the Decalogue following the *Shema*. They discontinued this, however, after the Christians attempted to make a point of the fact that it was the Decalogue rather than the *Shema* that God gave to Moses.

Christian scholars have consistently pointed out, however, that the synagogue gave the church a worship service that was centered on the reading and understanding of Scripture. It was set in the context of prayer and confession. It involved congregational participation and anticipated regular and frequent gathering.

That is rather significantly in contrast to the influence of Temple worship. It is hard to trace any continuity between Herod's Temple and the church. Jesus was frequently in Jerusalem at the feasts, paid the Temple tax, and expressed concern about its purity. But there is no evidence of His or the disciples' participation in the sacrifices. He advised the cleansed leper to go to the priest, and He expressed desire to eat the Passover with His disciples. Yet Stephen before the Sanhedrin (see Acts 7) saw no help to godliness in the presence of the Temple, and its destruction in A.D. 70 did not disrupt Christian worship.

It is significant that the synagogue was the first building specifically designed to house a congregation. That sense of local identity as a worshiping and learning community is also a contribution to Christian thinking and practice.

Contemporary Judaism

The Christian worshiper should be aware and appreciative of the past and present of Jewish worship. It is presently being acknowledged that our Christian churches have lost too much of the Jewishness that characterized them in the formative stage. However, Judaism itself has not remained static, and there are presently three widely divergent worshiping communities in America, and others in various places abroad.

The Orthodox Jews are the purists who take the Torah and Talmudic tradition as seriously as possible. They keep a *kosher* household (the word means "clean") by observing dietary regulations, and generally speaking, they resist the erosion of Jewish culture and isolation that has been underway since the rise of Reformed Judaism in the nineteenth century. Reformed Judaism was and is the deliberate attempt to modify the traditions so as to allow Jews to become a part of their culture (Western) without sacrificing ethical monotheism. It really differs very little in belief from unitarianism.

Between the two groups stands a third, the conservative Jews. These try to bridge the gap by "conserving" the Hebrew cult, the traditional services and observances, but at the same time allowing rather broad cultural adjustments. The service of worship in a Reformed synagogue would not vary all that much from many Protestant churches. Services in an Orthodox synagogue would be filled with Hebrew and traditional actions, and without assistance the observer would probably be unable to discern what was really going on. To any Christian, however, what will be most impressive in a Jewish service will be the reverence and excitement that are generated by the taking of the Scrolls from the ark and the procession with it through the congregation.

The advent of Christ brought many necessary changes to the form and content of worship that began with the traditions of the synagogue. The New Testament writings reveal some of those changes and how they affected the conversation between God and His people.

1. The dual purpose of the synagogue has its reflection in the church. How do you relate those purposes to your church?
2. Your appreciation of Christian worship would be enriched by a visit to a synagogue. You would be welcomed, but your ability to follow the service would depend on which of the three groups you attended. Many will have been in a Jewish wedding or a Bar or Bat Mitzvah. Share your experiences.
3. Consider inviting a rabbi or a cantor to visit your group and discuss synagogue worship.
4. Seder (Passover) services are being studied more and more, and often they are adapted for Christian groups during the Holy Week. You might help bring about such a project.
5. Read Luke 4:16–20; Acts 15:21; 18:4; and James 2:1–4. Discuss how these passages show historical continuity between Jewish and Christian worship.

4

Worship in the New Testament: Reading, Preaching, and Praying

We now come to what has to be the very heart of our study. No group of Christians attempts to understand or order its worship without some kind of appeal to the teaching or practice of the Christians in the New Testament. That is not as simple a matter as it might seem, but we will try to walk through the material in a clarifying and helpful way.

The Words for Worship

We noted that in the Old Testament the word primarily used for worship means "to fall down" or "to prostrate oneself toward." The same is true in the New Testament. *Proskuneō* means "to kiss (presumably the hand or the ground) toward." There is a similar word, used in Matthew 15:9, that means "to venerate or fear" (*sebomai*).

There are two words that may be translated either "worship" or "service." One we have already noted, *leitourgia*, which is the root of our word "liturgy." It is used in Luke 1:23; Acts 13:2; 2 Corinthians 9:12 and elsewhere. Paul, in Romans 15:16, was a *leitourgos* of Christ Jesus for the Gentiles, doing the "priestly work" of the gospel. In Philippians 2:30, Paul spoke of the "service" (*leitourgia*) that the Philippians had rendered him through Epaphroditus. In Philippians especially, Paul used the language of worship in a broad and inclusive sense. In 2:17 he said he was "poured out" (as a libation, a ceremonial pouring) over the "sacrifice and service" (*leitourgia*) of their faith.

The other word for service is *latreia*, and it occurs frequently as an equivalent of the Old Testament term, "service." A distinction worth noting is that in the Greek version of the Old Testament, *latreia* is used to translate the service of the cult, the worship of the people, but *leitourgia* is used for the work of the priests. In the New Testament that distinction is not maintained. In fact, the service of God, though cultic at times, is ultimately the entire life of the worshiping Christian. Romans 12:1-2 is the classic verse regarding that truth, which we shall consider shortly.

Teaching About Worship

We have mentioned the words first because they are probably closer to a "teaching" about worship than anything else in the New Testament. There is an amazingly small amount of material that conveys specific ideas or principles about worship. It isn't hard to understand that the church was made up of people who did indeed worship and who had great joy and fulfillment in doing so. It would hardly seem necessary to give forth with much philosophy or theology about it. In fact, the New Testament is not that kind of collection. Yet there are a few verses that should be cited.

The first is the classic statement of Jesus in John 4:23-24: "The hour is coming, and now is, when the true worshipers will worship the Father in spirit and truth, for such the Father seeks to worship him. God is spirit, and those who worship him must worship in spirit and truth."

It is important to notice that Jesus settled the question quickly as to whether worship can be restricted to a place or time. He also emphasized the Father's deep concern for worship being based on truth, and the necessity of worshiping in the Spirit. There is really no more significant text in the Bible on worship than this. There must be in worship an orthodoxy both of doctrine and of spiritual life.

We mentioned Paul's very inclusive and challenging

statement in Romans 12:1–2: "I appeal to you therefore, brethren, by the mercies of God, to present your bodies as a living sacrifice, holy and acceptable to God, which is your spiritual worship." This is the reading of the Revised Standard Version. The King James Version reads, "your reasonable service." It is a difficult phrase.

The word "reasonable," or "spiritual," is in the Greek *logikos*, which is from the word *logos* ("word" or "reason"). It occurs frequently in philosophical works and there it means "rational." In this passage, as in 1 Peter 2:2 ("The sincere [*logikos*] milk" KJV), it is obviously a contrast to the physical or material aspect, and is in a Christian setting, therefore, spiritual instead of rational.

But the word for worship is *latreia*, the word that does relate to the service of another but is so frequently employed to describe the service of worship. That idea is reinforced by Paul's use of "living sacrifice," a liturgical idea that is given an all-embracing quality. Just as the inanimate creation speaks the praise of God in Psalm 19, so the Christian can offer up to God all the events and actions of life. Our bodies are the vehicles of all our thoughts, words, and acts. A body presented to God is a holy, acceptable expression of the will of God and helps to fill the great anthem of praise and worship that properly rises to God from the entire created universe.

First Peter 2:9–12 reminds us that the existence of the church as a kingdom of priests is for the purpose of offering spiritual sacrifices acceptable to God through Jesus Christ, "that you may declare the wonderful deeds of him who called you out of darkness into his marvelous light" (v. 9). Worship, therefore, has no greater purpose, and no need of any other purpose, than to praise and magnify God. Ephesians 1:3–14 expresses the same idea: "we who first hoped in Christ have been destined and appointed to live for the praise of his glory" (v. 12).

Most of the teaching about worship in the New Testament is derived from various regulations and corrections that seemed to be necessary in the various churches. Paul was concerned about the conduct of the Corinthians at the Lord's Supper and wrote about that in 1 Corinthians 10 and 11. Although he did not mention it at all in the other Epistles, the Lord's Supper was probably celebrated by all the New Testament Christians and no needed correction.

The writer of Hebrews was concerned about attendance at the services and counseled the Christians not to be lax about it (see Heb. 10:25). James reminded the Christians that in their gatherings there could be no place for partiality. (The terminology is interesting: "For if a man...comes into your assembly [Gr. "synagogue"]..." James 2:2.)

Another source of information about worship in the New Testament that might easily be overlooked is the Book of Revelation. Over and over again there are scenes of the divine worship of Christ and of God the Father. Worship as the major occupation of heaven was seen earlier in Isaiah 6 and it is confirmed in the Apocalypse of John. John wrote of his own worship in chapters 1 and 22. He described the worship of the elders and living creatures in chapters 4 and 5, and that of the great multitude of the redeemed in chapters 7, 15, and 19.

Cultic Activity—What New Testament Christians Did

What we are really observing in the lack of "teaching" about worship in both the Old and New Testaments is an example of the way in which our theology comes to us. We are not so much given a body of truth as we are told what happened. Admittedly, part of the happening is teaching and instruction. Yet we are encouraged to learn as much from history as from discourse.

The problem with the record in the New Testament is

that we might be tempted to duplicate the record rather than be instructed by it. There has been a constant and proper drive within the life of the church to return to "New Testament Christianity." That is well-meaning and can be wholesome. Yet it can also be restrictive and unproductive. The church today should be what God wants the church to be today. Some of that configuration may look very much like a New Testament church, but some of it must look very different.

Some of it will be very much like the church of earlier times and places. If we believe that the Holy Spirit has guided the church in its pilgrimage through the centuries, then we must take seriously what the judgments and the practices of the church have been, especially if they have characterized Christians "at all times and in all places." That is why, in a later chapter, we will pay such careful attention to the early church, which was by and large a single entity and spoke its collective mind through the "ecumenical councils."

We must always keep asking ourselves whether the gospel, which Jesus described as new wine that constantly threatens old wineskins, has now become old wine that stays quite well in any skin, new or old. It shall now be our project to look at what the New Testament Christians did when they gathered to worship.

Reading the Scripture

We have already noted the synagogue service and the place it had for reading and exposition. Luke 4:16–27 and Acts 13:14–16 refer to that custom. Paul also mentioned the reading of the "Old Covenant" as an Israelite practice of his day (see 2 Cor. 3:14–15). It would seem only natural that Christians would continue the practice.

And they did. In 1 Timothy 4:13 the young church

leader was advised not to neglect the "public reading of Scripture." Paul added to that pastoral responsibility exhortation and teaching, which probably flowed right out of the reading.

There is other interesting biblical evidence regarding reading of the apostles' memoirs, which, of course, became the New Testament canon. Paul's writing was regarded by the apostle Peter as equal to "other scriptures" (see 2 Pet. 3:15-16). Paul himself gave instructions that his letters were to be read to the gathered churches (see Col. 4:16; 1 Thess. 5:27; Philem. 2). There may be some indication of this same expectation for public readings of the Gospels. That is most likely the background for the curious parentheses in Matthew 24:15 and Mark 13:14: "Let the reader understand." Jesus was warning His listeners of the desolation spoken of by Daniel. The prophet Daniel was consistently read aloud in the synagogue. Jesus did not write or speak that word; the admonition was from the Gospel authors to the person doing the "reading aloud," the cantor or public readers of the Scripture in the assembly.

Reading the Scripture aloud is almost implied in Revelation 1:3, where both reader and hearers are promised a blessing. We have no trouble at all, then, seeing as quite prominent the practice of Scripture reading in the worship or liturgy of the New Testament church.

Preaching

If the Jewish pattern was influential at all, preaching was as naturally a part of the worship service of the early church as the reading. The Book of Acts is filled with preaching, and, of course, Jesus and the disciples had been preachers of the Kingdom of God (see Acts 2:14-29; 3:12-26; 4:8-12; 10:36-43; and especially 13:16-41). Yet, of all of the above references to preaching, none are in the context of the gathered church. All are what could be called evangelistic or gospel preaching, given for the purpose of bringing to faith in Christ those who had not known the good news. That is the kind of preaching to which Paul referred in Romans 10:14: "And how are they to hear without a preacher?" and in 1 Corinthians 1:21: "For ... it pleased God through the folly of what we preach to save those who believe." Just as Jesus preached to the people in many settings, so the apostles and the early Christians went everywhere "preaching the gospel" (see Luke 9:6; Acts 8:25).

But what about preaching in the community of faith in the context of worship itself? We can start with an assumption. If there had been preaching in the synagogue by the Jews, and evangelistic preaching by the apostles, why would there not be a continuation of this in the church? To be sure, there are a couple of glimpses in Acts. There was daily instruction by Paul at Ephesus in the "School of Tyrannus." Paul probably rented the facility during the lengthy traditional daily siesta, and this continued, we're told, for two years (see Acts 19:8–10). In Acts 20:7–11, Paul was at Troas and spoke until midnight on the first day of the week, "when we were gathered together to break bread" (v. 7). It was there that Eutychus fell two stories to the ground and became the first serious warning to all worshipers to stay awake in church. Other interpretations suggest it is an admonition for all long-winded preachers!

It would be advantageous to develop at this point a statement on the New Testament theology of preaching. Preaching, or proclamation (the words often used are from the Greek kĕrux, "a herald or announcer," and kĕrygma, "the announcement or proclamation"), is itself a part of the work of the Holy Spirit whereby people are called into the Kingdom. It is a means or vehicle of God's grace. It is not so much that the preacher is talking about God; preaching is God talking through the messenger, and in that spoken word God calls and saves. Preaching is a primary means by which Christ's sheep hear His voice. It was always assumed in the Scriptures that the gospel (*evangel*) would be shared by preaching. And one word for preaching is evangelizing, giving out the good news.

We must be careful at this point, however, not to equate the proclamation of the gospel simply with a sermon by a pastor. There is far too much evidence in the New Testament to allow us to restrict the saving work of Christ in a proclaimed word to just a sermon by a preacher. Romans 10:14 asks the question, "How are they to hear without a preacher?" and the word there is *kērux*, "one who announces." The word is in no sense restricted to a title or an office. All Christians are called to proclaim the good news. On the other hand, it does not mean that some will not be gifted by the Spirit, called and ordained to proclaim the word authoritatively in behalf of God and His church. In such a case it is all the more essential to recognize that in that proclamation God is doing His work, giving His word, speaking and encountering humanity yet once more.

It is also important for us to note that preaching evidently takes on the additional role of teaching as it finds expression in the Christian community. Teaching in Greek is *didachē*, from which we get our term "didactic." The twofold aspect of evangelizing and teaching was a new development in the Christian community that had not been present in Jewish worship. The *kērygma* ("proclaimed good news of Christ") was a call to decision, to conversion. No Jew had been called by a preacher to "be converted" until John the Baptist. And no one was called to faith in the risen Christ until Pentecost. This did not mean that Jews were not called to repent, have faith in God, and walk humbly with Him. But the Christian preacher was calling on all people to repent and believe the good news of Christ. That done, baptism administered, and the believer then part of the Christian community, the role of preaching became largely teaching.

The gospel, of course, continues to make its call in the church to radical discipleship. We evangelical Christians have often failed to reckon with the "ongoing conversion" that is being asked by Christ at every point in our lives. Even to the Christian community the gospel call for decision keeps resounding. The presence of *kērygma* in all aspects of preaching, even in what might be termed teaching, should never be overlooked. This is really to say that all true preaching by the very name is kerygmatic, calling the Christian hearer to further decision.

We are all lifelong catechumens. There may well be a kind of "teaching" in the church that is in the Jewish tradition of Torah—largely concerned with the accurate transmission of a content or a tradition. Yet given the purpose of Christian teaching, it is hard to allow the material to become merely factual and the teacher to be dispassionate. We must move beyond the goal of getting Bible doctrine in our frontal lobes and seek to obey and live out God's holy word.

How do we deal with the fact that preaching is never listed as one of the gifts of the Spirit in the New Testament whereby the church will be built up? In 1 Corinthians 14:3 Paul wrote that a "prophet" speaks to build up, encourage (or exhort, the same word as in 1 Tim. 4:13), and console. That does sound like a kind of pastoral preaching, does it not? In 1 Corinthians 14:26 Paul noted that when the church came together each one had a hymn (psalm), a lesson or teaching (*didachē*), a revelation, a tongue, and interpretation. His appeal was for order, but the mention of teaching seems significant. In his list of gifts in Ephesians 4:11–12, he seemed to group pastors and teachers into one, so that the pastoral gift and office were tied to an ability and responsibility to teach.

New Testament scholars have worked at length to try to sort out the content of *kērygma* and *didachē,* proclamation and teaching. But it never quite works. There is a dynamic of the Holy Spirit in operation that defies neat categories. In the New Testament period, the corporate worship of the church was rooted above all else in the reading and proclamation of an apostolic, dynamic word. That word brought life and growth to the hearer because it was the word of Christ (see Col. 3:16), whether based on the Old Testament or derived from the apostles and prophets of Christ.

Praying

Nothing is more basic to worship—public or private—than prayer. It goes without saying that prayer was fundamental to the worship of the New Testament period. Our task, however, of understanding how worship has been expressed, and what Christian worship is all about, will be helped by a look at what changes in prayer took place in the first century itself. There are some elements that were taken from the Hebrew tradition of prayer, but there were also Christian additions.

The Hebrew Tradition of Prayer

The Jews usually stood to pray, often with upraised hands. They most likely also raised their faces toward heaven. The humility of the tax collector in Luke 18:13 was shown by the fact that he wouldn't "lift up his eyes." Acts 20:36 describes Paul and the Ephesian elders kneeling together in prayer on the shore at Miletus before his departure, and Paul wrote of bowing his knees in prayer for the Ephesians (see Eph. 3:14).

Times or hours of prayer, so basic to the spiritual life of

the Jews, were also observed by the Christians. Acts 3:1, for example, mentions the visit of Peter and John "at the hour of prayer, the ninth hour." We have already observed that the Jews in the synagogue prayed at the third, sixth, and ninth hours (9:00 A.M., noon, and 3:00 P.M.) and repeated the *Shema* at the time of morning and evening sacrifice. There is no mention of any specific gathering of the church at specified times other than on the first day of the week, nor even specific instructions as to times of prayer for private devotion. But like fasting ("when you fast . . . " Matt. 6:16), it would seem the New Testament writers assumed the hours of prayer would continue to be observed ("when you pray . . . " Matt. 6:6), for in the period immediately after the apostolic era, observing the hours of prayer was practiced throughout the church.

The forms of prayer continued in a Hebrew pattern as well, especially the use of the term *blessed*. That expression of praise and thanksgiving appears again and again. James warned us that the same tongue should not bless God and curse men (James 3:9). Blessing God is undoubtedly the equivalent of praising or even of thanking God. Yet when we bless the Lord we are in a sense sharing fully whatever good we have to give. It demands our full involvement, "all that is within me, bless his holy name!" (Ps. 103:1). Blessing also serves to bring a kind of announcement of worship or doxology into the picture. The praise and glory of God are kept in a primary position.

The concerns of prayer also follow the lines of Hebrew usage. There are not only praise and thanksgiving, but also intercession for the new Israel, the church. There are prayers for guidance (see Acts 1:14,24) and special intercession for the apostles when they are in danger (see Acts 4:23–31). It is interesting to note that the prayer of the faithful in Acts 4 is for boldness and steadfastness to witness in the midst of opposition rather than for release from their foes. Even Paul's command to intercede for those in authority (see 1 Tim. 2:2-4) was given so that the gospel might advance rather than merely being a desire for tranquility as an end in itself. Paul asked also for intercession on his behalf (see Rom. 15:30-31) but again it was for the success of his endeavors for the gospel rather than for purely personal affairs.

Another Hebrew practice of prayer that was continued in the church was the *Amen*. We have already noted its Old Testament usage. One writer telling of the huge crowd in attendance at a synagogue in Alexandria reported that a flag was waved at the appropriate times so all could join in the *Amen!* Paul complained that some in Corinth were praying in such a way that a person (especially an outsider) could not understand and therefore would not be able to join in the *Amen* (see 1 Cor. 14:16). There are *Amens* attached to many prayers and doxologies in the New Testament. In one beautiful passage (see 2 Cor. 1:20ff) Jesus Himself is described as the "yes" to the promises of God, and through Him we say Amen. The word is an affirmation, "So be it," and the Christians used it, as did the Jews, as a means of expressing their approval and involvement as a congregation. Abuse of its usage has led many churches today to drop it. Most churches using the liturgies from ancient tradition, however, are careful to keep it.

Christian Expression

When we ask what happened to prayer in the Christian community that made it different from the Jewish practices, we are immediately struck with one central answer—Jesus Christ Himself. Prayer is still essentially the address of the believing person to God. But into that prayer has come the overpowering magnificence of the Lord Jesus Christ. We can see this influence in three different ways.

First, there is the influence of the *person* of Christ. So

strongly is His presence a reality that very early we can see the inclination to address prayer to Christ rather than just to God the Father. Understandably, this is largely seen in brief, almost abrupt statements. Stephen, when dying, prayed, "'Lord Jesus, receive my spirit'" (Acts 7:59). There is also the unusual prayer that is preserved in the Aramaic, *Maranatha* (see 1 Cor. 16:22). The prayer seems to be repeated in Revelation 22:20 when it reads, "Come, Lord Jesus!" The phrase as it stands in Aramaic could mean "Our Lord comes," or if it is made *Marana tha* it would mean, "Our Lord, come." In either case it is a prayer that seems to be a part of corporate worship. A first-century document we will look at, the *Didache*, or the "Teaching of the Twelve Apostles," will repeat this phrase.

The New Testament use of the term *Lord*, referring both to God as quoted from the Old Testament and to Jesus Christ, is somewhat ambiguous. We could not arbitrarily say that the church in Antioch was directing itself to Jesus when it is said that they "were worshiping the Lord" (Acts 13:2). Paul said he besought "the Lord" three times regarding his thorn in the flesh and was told, "My grace is sufficient for you" (2 Cor. 12:8–9). Most of us would assume he addressed Jesus. The fact is, all three persons in the Holy Trinity are properly called Lord, for all fully share the divine nature and reign over heaven and earth together.

It is easy to understand how prayer centered upon Christ would come quite naturally to the worshiping church, for He, the eternal Son of the Father, assumed human flesh and dwelt among them. It is probably from the worship of the church that the reality of the full deity of Christ and the recognition of God as Father, Son, and Holy Spirit were finally discerned as the true apostolic and biblical faith. Those Christians knew that it was right to address Jesus in prayer long before they had worked out the philosophical and theological results of such activity.

Further, prayer in the presence of Christ was certainly the expectation of the church. Long after His ascension, the New Testament church was experiencing His presence. The classic promise for this is Matthew 18:19–20: " . . . if two of you shall agree on earth as touching any thing that they shall ask, it shall be done for them of my Father which is in heaven. For where two or three are gathered together in my name, there am I in the midst of them" (KJV).

Most scholars will point out that there is an earlier rabbinic statement that is quite similar: "If two sit together and the words of the Law are spoken between them, the Shekinah (the glorious presence) rests between them." However, it is now Jesus Himself who promises His presence, and His presence means that the concern of their prayer is known and heard.

It is tragic that there is not more emphasis on this promise of Christ in relation to our modern worship. There is here what might be called the sacrament of gathering, and Christ's "there am I" comes close to "this is my body." There is certainly a "Real Presence" promised to the church that she should properly fear to ignore.

The second way in which the prayers of the New Testament church were affected by Jesus is that He specifically *taught* them to pray, including the instruction to pray "in my name" (see Matt. 18:10–20; John 14:13; 15:16; 16:24,26). Later, Paul made it evident that the church did indeed follow Jesus' instruction (see Rom. 1:8; Col. 3:17; Eph. 5:20).

Jesus gave a great many instructions regarding prayer, but His teaching was largely for personal or private prayer rather than for corporate worship as such. The Gospel of Luke is filled with parables from Jesus that encourage us to pray persistently, with faith, and with humility. The Sermon on the Mount (see Matt. 5—7) counsels us to pray in secret, to pray with confidence, to pray briefly, and to pray to a Father who loves and hears us. The Lord taught the Twelve to pray personally, enabling them to teach the church to pray corporately (see Acts 2:47).

The Lord's Prayer (see Matt. 6:9–13; Luke 11:2–4) is absolutely central to Jesus' teaching concerning prayer. He offered it in response to a question from the disciples. While the prayer is not repeated in Acts or the Epistles, before the end of the first century (again in the *Didache*) the Christians were privately praying the prayer three times a day. It is so obviously a prayer intended for corporate worship (*Our* Father) that the church everywhere used it in that way. I find that an increasing number of evangelical churches are using the Lord's Prayer again in their worship and that Christians are rediscovering it for use in personal prayer. It is interesting, and perhaps demonstrates the freedom from rigidity and formula as ends in themselves, that the Lord's Prayer is not prayed in the name of Jesus.

The Christian tradition that according to many is the single most significant contribution of Jesus Christ to our understanding of prayer is the third factor: God is addressed as *Father*. The term is in the Lord's Prayer, but the heart of the teaching is in Jesus' use of the Aramaic *Abba* in the prayer in Gethsemane (see Mark 14:32–39). The Aramaic form is preserved, along with the Greek translation. Paul used the same term in Romans 8:15 and Galatians 4:6, again with a Greek translation for those who would not know the Aramaic, for the Greek *Pater* does not convey the same intimacy as the Aramaic.

There is no evidence that the Jews ever used *Abba* in addressing God. Variations on *Ab* are used, but they are the equivalent of "Our Father," not the tender and personal *Abba*, which approximates "Papa," or "Daddy." Even Paul, in putting the Greek beside the Aramaic, made no attempt to clarify or elaborate on *Abba*. Thus, the Christian church preserved the use of *Abba* as initiated by Jesus. To pray

"Our Father" for the Christian was understanding the relationship with God as personal. This was a great change from the Jewish view that God was the Father of Israel—the Patriarch—but hardly "my Father," whom one could address with domestic familiarity.

That dimension of Jesus' teaching on prayer should serve as a constant balance between an exclusively corporate mentality about our relationship to God and an excessive individualism. On the one hand, we pray to *our* Father, and we are never really alone in our address to God. But He is also a personal Father to all who believe—indeed, the God who lives in our hearts.

Perhaps Jesus' greatest influence on the prayer of the church came from the obvious priority He placed upon it. It has often been pointed out that Jesus prayed at every significant juncture in His life. Thus, His teaching is filled with counsel and instruction to us to pray at all times (see Luke 3:21; 6:12; 9:28; 22:39–45; 23:46). The true worshipers in the New Testament were those who prayed together in obedience to their Lord.

From the New Testament, then, we can see that one of the major changes in worship was in the emphasis on the spiritual dimension. Where the Jews worshiped by offering sacrifices and holding feast days, the New Testament Christians offered themselves as living sacrifices (see 1 Pet. 2:2,9–12) and celebrated the Lord's Supper in memory of the supreme sacrifice of Christ. Where synagogue worship offered the forms of Scripture reading, preaching, and prayer, the New Testament church filled those forms with the knowledge of Christ's presence in their midst. Most importantly, Jesus' call to corporate and personal prayer was a call to join with Him in an ongoing dialogue that would inform every aspect of church life. The New Testament church developed other forms in response to that call, and those we shall examine in the next chapter.

STUDY GUIDE

1. How does a careful reading of John 4:23–24 affect your ideas about worship?
2. How do you approach the "public reading of Scripture"? What commends it? What makes it ineffective? (Read Acts 13:14–16; 2 Cor. 3:14–15; 1 Tim. 4:13.)
3. What do you think is the relationship of "public reading" and the availability of Bibles for a congregation? Should you read or listen when the Bible is read?
4. From the New Testament evidence, what seems to be the role of preaching for the gathered community?
5. What has been your experience of prayer in corporate worship? How do you regard the use of the Lord's Prayer?

5

New Testament Worship: Specific Christian Developments

Sacraments

Jesus' ministry and teachings gave rise to a new set of ceremonial actions for the Christian church. Those actions, like the ones we discussed in the last chapter, were not necessarily new in themselves, but they took on new and sometimes altogether different meanings in the context of Christian worship.

Most Christians who do not accept the full witness and authority of church tradition perceive only two repeatable actions as being asked for by Jesus: the ceremonial use of water in baptism, and the eating and drinking of bread and wine, which we call the Lord's Supper or communion. We will look at both of those practices as they are revealed and taught in the New Testament, and we will have occasion to refer to them again many times as we proceed through the centuries of the worshiping church.

Historically, the term *sacrament* refers to those two actions. The word is from the Latin term used to translate the Greek word *musterion*, "mystery." For some Christians there is nothing mysterious at all about baptism and communion; they are often offended by the word. *Ordinance*, as something "ordered" by Christ, is the usual substitute. We will use the term *sacrament* because it is so universal in Christian discussion.

Baptism

There is nothing that directly corresponds to baptism in the Old Testament revelation except the frequent use of water for cleansing in the Temple ceremonies (see Lev. 15:5; 16:24,26; 17:15). The prophets taught of a moral cleansing for the coming age, signified by water (see Ezek. 36:25; Zech. 13:1; Is. 4:4). The New Testament writers, however, saw a link between those cleansing ceremonies and Christian baptism (see John 3:22–26; Heb. 6:2; 10:22).

The history of that linkage seems unquestionably to occur through the practice of the baptism of proselytes to Judaism and the baptism practiced by John. A proselyte was a Gentile who decided to become a Jew. There were two kinds. A "proselyte of the gate" was in sympathy with Jewish teaching and practice, attended worship in the synagogue, and prayed. A "proselyte of righteousness" was circumcised and baptized before assuming the full responsibility of Torah. The convert was a full participant in the faith. Baptism was part of the initiation into the fullness of the Jewish community. Men, women, and children were immersed in water and were considered, upon emerging from the water, to have entered a new life. The participant in that rite was usually naked—although the women were segregated and the rabbis read the Law aloud to them during the ceremony from a discreet distance.

It was against that background that John, the forerunner, began his unique ministry of baptizing. For baptism to represent moral renewal and cleansing was not new. But for someone to suggest that good practicing Jews needed the baptism of repentance was radically new. John also announced that his baptism was an act of preparation for the coming of the Kingdom of God (see Mark 1:4–5).

Upon the ministry of preparation and renewal Jesus placed His seal of approval by submitting Himself to John's baptism along with the crowds (see Matt. 3:15). His participation in the act was confirmed by miraculous signs: the heavens opened, God the Father spoke concerning His Son, and the Holy Spirit descended as a dove upon the obedient, well-pleasing Christ (see Matt. 3:16–17; John 1:29–34). For some time afterward, Jesus and His disciples continued their recognition of the baptizing that John had begun, although it is specifically stated that only the disciples, and not Jesus, were baptizing (see John 3:22; 4:1–2).

During His ministry Jesus twice used the word *baptism* (see Luke 12:50; Mark 10:38–39) to refer to His approaching suffering and death. This may be assumed to be the basis on which Paul later referred to water baptism as uniting us with the death of Christ (see Rom. 6:13; 1 Cor. 12:12). But the final words of Jesus in Matthew 28:19–20 constitute a single, clear-cut command to His disciples that they baptize His followers.

When we come to the Book of Acts we find baptism not only being administered, but also being included in the apostolic preaching of repentance (see Acts 2:38; 8:16, 35–38; 10:48; 19:5; 22:16). People heard, believed, and were baptized, in just that simple and direct a sequence. Baptism was, in some instances, accompanied by a laying on of hands and the gift of the Holy Spirit. This may have also included anointing with oil, but the evidence is not clear. Most scholars point out that the three realities of Christian initiation were repentance, baptism, and the gift of the Spirit. There was no automatic result from baptism, nor was there a consistency in the sequence. Cornelius received the Spirit and was then baptized (see Acts 10:44–48), as did Paul (see Acts 9:17–19). The Ephesians in Acts 19:5 had that order reversed.

Very little is said as to how baptism was administered. There was probably variety in this, as in many other aspects of worship. The consistent factor was the water. The earlier baptisms of John the Baptist and of some of the sects in Judaism would indicate that immersion was common, although there could also be effusion—baptism by pouring water on the person. Few will deny that John brought the crowds to the Jordan because there was adequate water for a ceremonial bath. It can be noted here that the word *baptizō* has just enough variation in its usage both in and out of Scripture to keep anyone from absolute dogmatism about its meaning.

The significance of baptism, however, is a rich and rewarding study. In the New Testament, the meaning of washing away sin is obvious (see Eph. 5:26; Titus 3:5; 1 Cor. 6:11). There is also significant emphasis on the idea of new life in Christ. That is very naturally associated with the death and resurrection of Jesus, and Paul's great use of the figure is in Romans 6:3-11. Similar teaching is found in Colossians 2:11-12, where Paul also claimed that we receive in Christ a spiritual circumcision. But he saw baptism as relating to union with Christ in death, not in His baptism in the Jordan. That idea stands close to a Pauline figure that may well have recalled baptism to his readers; "putting off" the old clothing of their sinful selves and "putting on" the garments of life in Christ (see Gal. 3:27; Col. 2:9-14) was symbolically enacted by the early Christians as part of the liturgy of baptism.

Two problems should be mentioned. One is the seeming disparity between the formula prescribed by Jesus in Matthew 28:19—baptism in the name of Father, Son, and Holy Spirit—and the phrase used in Acts and implied in Paul—baptism in the name of the Lord Jesus. The answer that seems most satisfactory is this: to the Jew, being baptized in the name of Jesus as Lord would be the essence of repentance and new commitment. The triune name, on the other hand, would guide Gentiles into the full understanding of the God they now served. Both formulas were evidently used at first, but the need for a Jewish formula gradually diminished.

The other problem is the seeming indifference of Paul in 1 Corinthians 1:14–17 to baptism. "Christ did not send me to baptize" were his words. In context, he was trying to undermine the party spirit of Corinth. He reminded them that they were not baptized in the name of Paul, and he was relieved that most of them could not take pride that he might have baptized them. But if baptism could be an excuse for sectarianism, its significance would be underscored. And Paul's other writing hardly allows us to say that baptism was in any way unimportant to him.

The point is, the church followed the example and the command of Christ and baptized believers and their families, including, most likely, small children. It does not seem questioned at all that baptism, the washing that answers to repentance and identification with Christ by faith, does indeed mark our initiation in the body of Christ. It is a true death to the old self, a resurrection to new life, and a sealing by the Holy Spirit, who indwells and directs the Christian. It is not magical, but neither is it meaningless. Something happens! Given the qualifications of repentance and faith that surround it, the reality that God pictures, He accomplishes.

The Lord's Supper

The other ceremonial action Christ established for His followers is the Lord's Supper. This is known by some as communion or Holy Communion, taken from 1 Corinthians 10:16. The Greek word for communion is *koinonia*, one we encounter frequently in the New Testament and in the historic church. Its basic meaning is "participation" or "sharing."

Another term for communion is Eucharist, derived from the Greek word *eucharistia*, which means "thanksgiving."

The term came to be used because the Lord Jesus Christ "gave thanks" as He took the bread and wine, and we do the same. The Orthodox church often refers to the Eucharist as "the Holy Mystery." The Roman Catholic term, *Mass*, also refers to the Eucharist, but includes more than that. *Mass* probably comes from the closing statement of the Eucharistic liturgy given by the priest: *Ite, missa est*— "Go, this is the dismissal."

There are three accounts of the Eucharist in the New Testament. One account is repeated and is virtually identical in two of the Gospels—Matthew 26:26-29 and Mark 14:22-25. The second is in Luke 22:15-19. The third is from Paul in 1 Corinthians 11:23-27, with some accompanying comments in 1 Corinthians 10:16-17. The differences in these accounts are of interest to the scholar, but the liturgical form of the Eucharist that emerges is fairly clear.

Jesus met with His disciples in the Upper Room. It was Passover time, and the Synoptic Gospels (Matthew, Mark, and Luke) imply that the disciples were eating the Passover meal. The room was prepared with the specific objective of "eating the Passover," and Jesus commented that He had earnestly desired to eat that Passover with His disciples (Luke 22:15). John's Gospel, however, indicates that Jesus was crucified at the time when the Passover lambs were being killed, which means that the meal in the Upper Room could not have been a regular Passover observance. (There has been long and inconclusive debate about this problem. The only tangible result, however, is whether or not to use unleavened bread. The Orthodox church follows John's Gospel and uses regular bread. Many Western churches have followed the Synoptics and use unleavened bread or wafers.) The Lord's Supper so quickly became a Christian event that its relation to the Passover becomes rather incidental.

From that meal Jesus selected (took) bread and wine. He gave thanks, broke the bread, and passed the cup of wine with a very brief explanation of their meaning. That is similar to the Jewish *Haggadah* (meaning "telling") at the Passover, the explanation by the father of the meaning of the meal. Jesus simply explained, "This is my body," and "this is my blood." The texts vary a bit on the second statement, some adding that the blood is the new covenant and is shed for the remission of sins. Jesus asked the disciples to "*do* this," for a remembrance or memorial of Him. Paul added, "as often as you drink it," showing that no specific command of frequency was known.

This is the "shape" of the liturgy, a term that is used frequently by students of worship to describe the basic format of the Eucharist. We are all aware of the wide range of controversy that has flowed around this event and its interpretations. Some of that we will look at as we proceed in our study. At this point we should emphasize the open and rather uncomplicated way in which the Eucharist is presented in the New Testament. It is an action, "Do this," with no prescription as to words to be said, or even how often. Eat bread and drink wine. It is a memorial, a remembrance of Christ.

The Greek word for remembrance is *anamnēsis*, and here we begin to move more deeply into theological waters. It must be admitted that this "remembering" has an intensity and depth that challenges us. It represents an event in such a way that the participant becomes part of the story. We touched on that idea when we described the scene at Passover (p. 29). It is not that something happens again as much as the idea that we move back into or relive the event. This, in part, is what many in the church mean when they refer to the Lord's Supper as a "sacrament" or mystery. The other focus for mystery has been the relationship of Christ's body and blood to the bread and wine.

More on that later. The disciples were certainly oblivious to any metaphysical, mysterious presence of Christ's body in the bread and wine when He first gave it to them, but that does not limit the meaning in the mind of Jesus.

We should note also that the supper was given a meaning for the future. In the Gospels Jesus commented that He would not drink the cup again until He drank it new with them in His Father's kingdom (see Matt. 26:29). Paul added that the feast would be kept "until he comes." Jesus had frequently used a banquet as the figure of the coming messianic kingdom (see Matt. 26:29) and that idea is repeated in Revelation 19:7-10.

Paul further informed his readers that in this action we "proclaim" the Lord's death. That gives an interesting and powerful facility to the ceremonial action of eating bread and drinking wine. The "word" of Jesus—His own explanation—is what makes clear the meaning and significance of the act. But when that is done, it is the act itself that finds a voice and proclaims—preaches—the "word" or message of the cross.

Acts and the Epistles by themselves do not supply us with evidence that the Eucharist was preeminent in the life of the church. Paul did not mention it to any church other than Corinth. The phrase "breaking of bread" occurs rather frequently in Acts, and it almost has to have liturgical significance. Acts 2:42 puts the phrase with the apostles' doctrine, fellowship, and prayers, and it could hardly mean that the new Christians just kept on eating. The same may be said for Acts 20:7, when the church had gathered together on the first day of the week to break bread. But Acts 27:33-35 has Paul breaking bread for the passengers of the ship, hardly a liturgical action. Yet, again, we must conclude that silence does not indicate neglect or absence. The Lord's Supper was most probably the regular activity of a church that was still so close in time to the events that gave rise to the ceremony.

The church was also close enough to the first event to have included the meal from which the Lord's Supper was taken. This was called the *Agapē* (a Greek word referring to unselfish love). The Gospels mention that the Eucharist took place "while they were eating," and Paul spoke of the cup as "after supper." It was that potluck dinner that created the problems at Corinth, and the practice died out in the early days of church history. There are perennial attempts to revive it, but the logistics make it difficult as a frequent event.

The New Testament material does not allow us to do guesswork about the significance of the Eucharist in the life of the church. Speculation proves interesting but not convincing. One scholar has tried to discern that the early Eucharists were joyous remembrances of the resurrected Christ, since that was very probably the situation for the resurrection appearance of Jesus. The disciples were back in the Upper Room. They undoubtedly ate, and that included bread and wine. They must have been filled with the painful, precious memory of their meeting there with Jesus but a few hours before and of His command to remember Him with bread and wine. Into that scene Jesus Himself came and blessed the disciples with His peace. Could they ever again eat bread and drink wine without remembering the joy of that occasion? Was that joyful remembrance of the Resurrection the background to the revelry at Corinth and Paul's necessary reminder that the proclamation was of Christ's death? This is conjecture, although we shall see that the church of the East (Orthodox) kept far more of this aspect of the Eucharist than the West.

We can say that the Eucharist was the unquestioned scene of the joyous meeting of Christ and His people. First

Corinthians 10:16–18 says that to eat and drink (the order there is drink and eat) is to participate (fellowship, share) in the body and blood of Christ, and that lips that have tasted heavenly food should not participate with demons by eating food from their altars.

The implication is clear. To sit at the Lord's Table was to have communion with Him, to share in His passion, including His life, death, and resurrection, and to eat the bread of the Kingdom of God. It was to invite Him to be present as He promised and to claim that presence as a promise and a guarantee of the coming kingdom of power and glory. And in spite of the complications from theological controversy, ecclesiastical regulations and restrictions, and many other evidences of human frailty, the Lord's Table has been the scene of sacred encounter for millions of Christ's people through the intervening centuries.

Hymns and Songs

One would suspect that if the worship life of the New Testament church was an experience of joy and spiritual vitality, it would be filled with singing. We have already seen that to be part of the history of Israel's worship, and the evidence is strong that the practice very naturally moved into and flourished within the church. The New Testament is a book of joy, a quality listed by Paul as a fruit of the Spirit second only to love (see Gal. 5:22). James assumed that singing was the language of joy: "Is any merry? let him sing psalms" (James 5:13 KJV).

It might have been the Old Testament Psalms that James had in mind, since those were so prominent in New Testament thought and life. The Gospel of Luke contains four songs in the first two chapters that borrow significantly in style and content from the Psalms. They have become known by their first words from the Latin text and have been used in worship from the earliest centuries.

1. *Magnificat*—Luke 1:46–55. Mary's psalm of praise for God's mighty work in and for her.
2. *Benedictus*—Luke 1:68–79. The song of Zacharias, father of John the Baptist.
3. *Gloria in excelsis*—Luke 2:14. The song of the angels (although it is not "sung" but "said") at the birth of Jesus.
4. *Nunc dimittis*—Luke 2:29–32. The song of Simeon after seeing Jesus: "Lord, now lettest thou thy servant depart in peace" (v. 29).

Three of these are very personal responses of praise for what God has done for the individuals involved. Their use by Christians through the centuries demonstrates that personal and communal piety stand very close together. The church readily utilizes what is essentially a personal experience.

We have described the above passages as songs or psalms because the New Testament does not attempt to distinguish them as poetic expressions of praise. In Colossians 3:16 and Ephesians 5:18–20, however, Paul spoke of the expression of the Spirit through "psalms and hymns and spiritual songs." The term *spiritual* should probably be applied to all three words, since it is from the Spirit that now those psalms, hymns, and songs will come. The word *psalm* is from the Greek and means "a song accompanied by a plucked instrument (harp)." *Hymn* is also Greek and means "a song addressed to a deity," but the words are not used with discrete meanings. Paul seems to have been referring to outbursts of song under the inspiration of the Spirit, which was also the object of his discussion of singing in 1 Corinthians 14:15.

It might be expected that the church would begin to develop its own hymnody as well as to utilize the great expressions of praise that the Old Testament provides. There are several passages that, by the poetic arrangement of words and phrases, seem to be hymns of the church. Ephesians 5:14 may well have been a baptismal hymn, "Awake, O sleeper, and arise from the dead, and Christ shall give you light." It isn't hard to hear that as a song.

There are four New Testament hymns that especially present the glory of the person and work of Christ. In each there is a statement about the preexistent Christ and about the incarnate and the glorified Christ. Just as in the Old Testament, however, we must admit that we have little idea of what the melodies were like, though probably the hymns were chanted. They appear as follows:

1. . . . though he was in the form of God, did not count equality with God a thing to be grasped, but emptied himself, taking the form of a servant, being born in the likeness of men. And being found in human form he humbled himself and became obedient unto death, even death on a cross. Therefore God has highly exalted him and bestowed on him the name which is above every name, that at the name of Jesus every knee should bow, in heaven and on earth and under the earth, and every tongue confess that Jesus Christ is Lord, to the glory of God the Father (Phil. 2:6–11).

2. He is the image of the invisible God, the first-born of all creation; for in him all things were created, in heaven and on earth, visible and invisible, whether thrones or dominions or principalities or authorities—all things were created through him and for him. He is before all things, and in him all things hold together. He is the head of the body, the church; he is the beginning, the firstborn from the dead, that in everything he might be pre-eminent. For in him all the fulness of God was pleased to dwell, and through him to reconcile to himself all things, whether on earth or in heaven, making peace by the blood of his cross (Col. 1:15–20).

3. He was manifested in the flesh,
      vindicated in the Spirit,
         seen by angels,
      preached among the nations,
      believed on in the world,
         taken up in glory (1 Tim. 3:16).

4. He reflects the glory of God and bears the very stamp of
   his nature, upholding the universe by his word of
   power. When he had made purification for sins, he sat
   down at the right hand of the Majesty on high (Heb.
   1:3).

Paul and Silas sang "hymns to God" at midnight in the
Philippian jail (Acts 16:25), and the prisoners listened to
them. Christ and the disciples sang a hymn before leaving
the Upper Room (see Matt. 26:30; Mark 14:26). It is assumed they sang part of the *Hallel*, Psalms 113–118, which
was sung at Passover, but that is not really known.

In the Book of Revelation, the scene in heaven is filled
with song. The hosts of heaven join the redeemed of all
ages and sing,

> Great and wonderful are thy deeds,
> O Lord God the Almighty!
> Just and true are thy ways,
> O King of the ages! (Rev. 15:3).

Confessions (Creeds)

One formula that evidently was frequently repeated in
New Testament worship was the brief statement, "Jesus is
Lord." Paul returned to this sentence frequently (see Rom.
10:9; 1 Cor. 12:3; 2 Cor. 4:5). It is easy to see how it would
act as a proper confession of Christian faith.

Paul also mentioned what might be a kind of creed in

1 Corinthians 15:3–5. He identified it as the "tradition"—
what had been delivered to him he now gave faithfully to
the Corinthians: ". . . that Christ died for our sins. . . , that
he was buried, that he was raised on the third day in accordance with the scriptures."

First Timothy 3:16 is a most intriguing passage in the
area of public confession. The word for confession introduces the verse, but it cannot be translated as a formal introduction. The Revised Standard Version reads, "Great
indeed, we confess, is the mystery of our religion." This
probably refers to a kind of "confession" in the church. To
see the verse that follows in Greek is quickly to recognize it
as a hymn (see example 3, previous section). There are six
verbs, all rhyming and forming into neat stanzas.

Confession is very properly associated with baptism, as
is clearly seen in Acts 8:35–38. Philip baptized the Ethio-
pian, and in some ancient manuscripts there is the statement in verse 37: "I believe that Jesus Christ is the Son of
God." The church fathers spoke of a threefold confession
of faith in God the Father, Son, and Holy Spirit as part of
baptism. We see in the New Testament a clear practice of
the use of the trinitarian formula in the Great Commission
(see Matt. 28:19). The formulation of such statements had
begun, and the confessional nature of the Christian faith
was becoming increasingly clear.

It is interesting that the New Testament does not record
any evidence of the confession of sin as part of corporate
worship, nor was there an equivalent synagogue tradition
from which the Christians might draw. First John 1:9 says,
"If we confess our sins, he is faithful and just, and will for-
give our sins and cleanse us from all unrighteousness." But
that is not restricted to the gathered church. James 5:16
speaks of confessing our sins to each other that we may be
healed, but again there is no liturgical setting. Perhaps it is
fair to say that the Christian community was so aware of

itself as a people who had been reconciled and forgiven that it gathered to proclaim and celebrate that reality. In any case, there is no clear evidence that the church did *not* make corporate confession.

Other Characteristics of New Testament Worship

What general characteristics of worship emerge in addition to the specific New Testament practices we have examined?

1. *The Presence of Christ.* We have already stated that the great innovation of Christian worship is the influence of the teaching and presence of the person of Christ. The church gathered for fellowship with her risen Lord (see Matt. 18:19–20). If we could continue to worship in that profound awareness, it alone would transform us. Everything we do in worship has the potential of making us aware of Christ's presence, thus making worship a vital and exciting experience. We are reminded of His presence in using Jesus' name in prayer, praise, and thanksgiving, in reciting the apostles' recollections of the life and teachings of Jesus, in being baptized in obedience to Jesus, and in celebrating the Lord's Supper to remember Jesus. Worship is encountering Jesus, and this dynamic should always be the underlying rationale, motivation, and reality of worship.

2. *The Work of the Spirit.* Not only is Jesus present, the Holy Spirit is present. Jesus taught that true worship is in the Spirit (see John 4:24) and Paul, in Philippians 3:3, said, "We . . . worship by the Spirit of God." Virtually all the activity and significance of Christ in worship is said to occur through the power of the Spirit. Prayer is generated and mediated by the Spirit (see Rom. 8:26–27; Eph. 6:18); praise is given in the Spirit (see 1 Cor. 14:2,15); the Word of God is understood by the Spirit (see 1 Cor. 2:10–16); confession of Jesus as Lord is by the Spirit (see 1 Cor.

12:3); and the Spirit is the source of gifts that edify the church (see 1 Cor. 12 and 14).

The New Testament introduces into Christian worship the encouraging and inspiring work of the Holy Spirit, who moves in and through all aspects of the praise, prayer, and celebration of the community to create an open way between our God and His worshiping church.

3. *Spontaneity and Variation.* The contrast between New Testament worship and that of the Temple and synagogue is the new enthusiasm and *participation* by the congregation. Those aspects flow from the work of the Spirit, which we have just noticed. Spontaneity seems an appropriate reflection of the breadth and freedom of the work of the Spirit. The excitement of the newly formed church was that the Spirit had come upon all—young and old, men and women, Jew and Gentile—and in that new community God was using all kinds of people as vehicles for His praise and work. The context was that of the amazing freedom in regard to form, but it did not negate a concern for order (see 1 Cor. 14:40).

Paul did seek to bring a kind of regulation to the Corinthians. Yet that was so that the gifts of the Spirit could be expressed, not repressed. The eagerness and ability to make a contribution to the worship were the problem, the kind of problem that a great many churches would dearly love to have. It is to be expected that the initial enthusiasm will be tempered when the church becomes established and develops a tradition. The problems of spontaneity were already making themselves felt in Corinth. Yet it is important to get a firm grasp of the initial thrust of Christian worship. Change is inevitable, but change is destructive if it is not based on understanding.

The New Testament church's spontaneity had its corresponding inevitable variety. There is no fixed pattern of worship recorded in the New Testament. The churches had their "liturgies," but what form they took was not part of the essence of the gospel. Diversity may be reflected in the hymns of the New Testament.

Some scholars find an early Palestinian Jewish Christianity in the psalms of Luke, a Hellenistic Jewish Christianity in the hymns of Revelation, a more sophisticated form of the same in Philippians, Colossians, John, and Hebrews, and an even different variety of Hellenistic Christianity in 1 Timothy and 1 Peter. Such diversity arises when worship is allowed to reflect the moods and background of a particular group of worshipers. They use their own language and thought forms to express themselves most meaningfully. That phenomenon is ever-present and, strangely enough, is still rather accurately shown in the hymnody of a particular group. Diversity in worship, therefore, is not depicted as evil in the New Testament, although we have already seen a consistent expectation in the recognition of the centrality of Christ and the work of the Spirit.

4. *Edification.* We have already met that word. New Testament Christians believed that proper worship would result in their being strengthened in their faith and equipped for their service. We may decide that edification is not the first reason for everything we do in worship, but a result of worship properly done will be to build us up in our Christian life. This is another way of saying that we may not go to church for what we can get out of it, but if we truly worship we cannot help getting something out of it.

5. *Word and Sacrament.* It is enough for us to say that New Testament worshipers gave place to the ministry of the Word and also to the observance of the sacraments, baptism and the Eucharist. There is no clear evidence that the Eucharist was always celebrated when they gathered. There is no clear indication of all that they said and did either at baptism or at the Eucharist. But it is obvious that

those events took place and were important.

It is also obvious that the church grew as it was instructed in the Word of God. The Old Testament was the basis of apostolic preaching, and quickly the writings of the apostles and the gospel story of the life, death, and resurrection of Jesus took their place of importance as the Word of God for the new Israel.

From the church's beginnings, then, we can see the development of some specific activities such as baptism and the Lord's Supper, as well as an ongoing use of older forms that had been passed on from Old Testament and synagogue worship. All those activities were filled with the new knowledge and joy of Christ's presence and the work of the Holy Spirit. We have also observed the spontaneity and diversity in the practices and especially in the hymns of the first Christian churches.

Upon this basis, Christians of succeeding generations have built their traditions. In the next few chapters we shall see how the long march of Christ's people through the years has presented us with a heritage as rich as it is diverse. As we view the ways in which Christians have responded to the call of worship, we shall gain not only a better understanding of how we have arrived where we are today, but also we shall see new possibilities for enriching our own worship experience. We shall explore those possibilities in the final chapters.

STUDY GUIDE

1. There are a number of passages in both the Old and New Testaments about baptism. Look at those carefully.
2. What are the things signified in baptism?

3. What contribution to the worshiper should a service of baptism make? What do you think of a "private" baptismal service?

4. What attitudes and responses are most felt when you celebrate the Eucharist? Is this good or does it need attention?

5. How many things can you describe as dramatized or made real by the Eucharist?

6. Use the hymnal or a few church bulletins and notice the "hymns" (addressed to God) and the songs (addressed to ourselves). Perhaps you can find some that seem to fit both ideas.

7. What benefits, if any, can you see coming from the recitation of a creed? Below are the Apostles' Creed and the Nicene Creed. Examine them and comment.

The Apostles' Creed
I believe in God the Father Almighty, Maker of heaven and earth, and in Jesus Christ, His only Son, our Lord, Who was conceived by the Holy Ghost, born of the Virgin Mary, suffered under Pontius Pilate, was crucified, dead and buried; He descended into hell; the third day He rose again from the dead; He ascended into heaven and sitteth on the right hand of God the Father Almighty; from thence He shall come to judge the quick and the dead. I believe in the Holy Ghost, the Holy Catholic Church, the communion of saints, the forgiveness of sins, the resurrection of the body and the life everlasting. Amen.

The Nicene Creed
We believe in one God, the Father, the Almighty maker of heaven and earth, of all that is, seen and unseen. We believe in one Lord, Jesus Christ, the only Son of God, eternally begotten of the Father, God from God, Light from Light, true God from true God, begotten, not made, of one Being with the Father. Through him all things were made. For us and for our salvation he came down from heaven: by the power

of the Holy Spirit he became incarnate from the Virgin Mary, and was made man. For our sake he was crucified under Pontius Pilate; he suffered death and was buried. On the third day he rose again in accordance with the Scriptures, he ascended into heaven and is seated at the right hand of the Father. He will come again in glory to judge the living and the dead, and his kingdom will have no end. We believe in the Holy Spirit the Lord, the giver of life, who proceeds from the Father and the Son: With the Father and Son he is worshiped and glorified. He has spoken through the Prophets. We believe in one holy catholic and apostolic Church. We acknowledge one baptism for the forgiveness of sins. We look for the resurrection of the dead, and the life of the world to come. Amen.

6

Worship in the Ancient and Orthodox Church

As we begin our study of the development of worship traditions in the church, we must remember that although we do not know what happened to some segments of the church the preservation of certain material is an indication of how important it was. Also, it is probably representative of many people. We must be imaginative and realize that something we regard as odd might have been very meaningful to the people who practiced it.

In this section, we will look at some of our earliest sources regarding worship: (1) the *Didache*, an anonymous work from the beginning of the second century; (2) a teacher in the middle of the second century named Justin Martyr; and (3) a theologian who followed Justin by about fifty years, Hippolytus.

1. Worship Immediately Following the Apostolic Church: The Didache

"The Teaching of the Twelve Apostles," known also as the *Didache* (Greek meaning "teaching"), is of unknown date and authorship. Estimates range from A.D. 50 to A.D. 150, but most scholars assume the date to be around A.D. 70, in the heart of the apostolic era. The book contains sixteen sections that deal with numerous topics. The first six chapters are a discussion of "The Two Ways," "The Way of Life" and "The Way of Death," which seem to be a kind of moral catechism for those who were preparing for baptism. The later chapters are about the rites and office-bearers of the Christian community, and the work closes with an exhortation to watchfulness in preparation for the imminent return of Christ.

The worship information from the *Didache* that interests us relates to baptism, Lord's Day worship, and the Eucharist. It is the essence of simplicity. Baptism, the rite of initiation, is to be done in "living water," a spring or stream, if possible. Immersion is preferred, but where water is insufficient, affusion (pouring) is permissible. It is performed in the name of the Holy Trinity. Fasting beforehand is recommended.

Information about the Eucharist proves extremely interesting. Chapter 9 contains this instruction:

As for the Eucharist, give thanks like this.
First, for the cup:
We give thee thanks, our Father,
for the holy vine of David thy servant
that thou hast revealed to us through Jesus, thy Child.
Glory to thee forever!

Next, for the broken bread;
We give thee thanks, our Father,
for the life and the knowledge
that thou hast revealed to us through Jesus, thy Child.
Glory to thee forever!

Just as this bread which we break,
once scattered over the hills,
has been gathered and made one,
so may thy Church too be assembled
from the ends of the earth into thy kingdom!
For glory and power are thine forever.

No one is to eat or drink your Eucharist

Except those who have been baptized in the name of the
Lord;
for in this regard the Lord said:
"Do not give holy things to the dogs."

Chapters 11–13 discuss the prophets and attempt to
show the Christians that the ministry of local deacons and
presbyters is equally valid with that of the itinerant, and
often more impressive, prophets. Then a problem is posed
by a reopening of the instructions about the Eucharist.

And on the Lord's Day of the Lord come together and break
bread, and give thanks, after confessing your transgres-
sions, that your sacrifice may be pure. Let no one that hath
any dispute with his fellow come together with you, until
they be reconciled, that your sacrifice may not be profaned.

For this is that [Scripture] which was spoken by the Lord
[Mal. 1:11,14]: "In every place and time offer me a pure sacrifice: for I am a great King, saith the Lord, and my name is
marvelled at among the Gentiles."

Elect, therefore [to see this rule carried out], for yourselves
bishops and deacons worthy of the Lord ... for they too
minister to you the ministry [leitourgia] of the prophets and
teachers. Therefore, despise them not, for they are those
that are honored of you with the prophets and teachers.

The problem for us is the repeated instruction regarding
the Eucharist. Some help comes if the *Agapē* is considered
as in mind, but there are still difficulties. This would mean
a more liturgical instruction for the *Agapē* than for the Eucharist, which seems strange. But there are other points of
significance we must see.

The baptized were to participate in the Eucharist, although catechists (those being instructed) were expected to

be present. The service was a "sacrifice," as understood in Malachi 1:11. This is the first evidence of the term in the language of the Eucharist. It does not appear in the New Testament. It is neither in the institution narratives nor in 1 Corinthians 10, even though Paul was discussing the sacrifices of the pagans. The Passover festival did not involve a sacrifice, even though a lamb was killed. Paul did say in 1 Corinthians 5:7, "Christ our passover is sacrificed" (KJV), but that was not at all in a setting that related to the Eucharist.

However, it is not difficult to see how easily the term would move into the context of the Eucharist. Even the simple reality of remembering the death of Christ would remind the Christian of "sacrifice." Some scholars see in this statement of the *Didache* the beginning of the protracted controversy about the nature of the Eucharist. But the reference here is uncomplicated. The sacrifice is the prayer, praises, worship, and gifts of the believers. There is not the slightest hint of the possibility of its being the resacrifice of Christ.

There is no statement about the words of institution, and the prayers are suggested, but not required. The document also contains the directive that Christians repeat the Lord's Prayer three times a day, but specific times are not mentioned. The overall impression from the book is one of increased formalism, or at least form, in the worship life of the church.

It is instructive for us to note how quickly the church found it necessary to order matters that related to its worship. That was not done in any spirit of rigidity. The church was concerned that it retain authentic worship practices, and above all else it wanted people to understand the significance of its liturgy and receive their full measure of edification from it. That responsibility is still with us.

2. Justin Martyr

Justin was born in Samaria, lived in Ephesus, and then went to Rome where he was a teacher of Christian doctrine. His "Dialogue with Trypho" is a clear and persuading account of an earnest seeker who finds satisfaction in Christian truth.

In about A.D. 155 he wrote the *Apology I*. In it he used the Greek word *apologia* in its meaning of "a defense or answer," not our normal modern usage of the word to mean "a begging of pardon." In the last seven chapters he described Christian worship, which was much maligned and misunderstood in the Roman world. He gave two accounts of the Eucharist, one that followed a baptism and one that followed a service of reading the Word and preaching.

In summary, the newly baptized person was escorted into the "assembly of those who are called brethren," and he joined in the prayers that were offered. The "kiss of peace" followed, then bread and a cup of water mingled with wine were presented to the "president" of the brethren. He offered thanksgiving "at some length," and the people shouted the *Amen*. Then all partook.

Justin then gave an explanation of the "eucharistized" bread and wine as the flesh and blood of the incarnate Jesus, as recorded by the apostles in their account of Jesus' command, "Do this for my *anamnēsis* [remembrance]." Justin next commented on the way the rich came to the aid of the poor and described a Sunday service:

On the day which is called Sunday, all who live in the cities or in the countryside gather together in one place. And the memoirs of the apostles or the writings of the prophets are read as long as there is time. Then, when the reader has finished, the president, in a discourse, admonishes and invites the people to practice these examples of virtue. Then we all stand up together and offer prayers.

And, as we mentioned before, when we have finished the prayer, bread is presented, and wine with water; the president likewise offers up prayers and thanksgivings according to his ability, and the people assent by saying, Amen. The elements which have been "eucharistized" are distributed and received by each one; and they are sent to the absent by the deacons. Those who are prosperous, if they wish, contribute what each one deems appropriate ... Sunday, indeed, is the day on which we all hold our common assembly.

It is an encouragement and a delight to find the Christians of more than eighteen centuries ago engaged in the very words and actions that are so familiar to us who love Christ today.

3. The Apostolic Tradition of Hippolytus

This theologian of Rome became a bishop in about A.D. 217. His writing has received renewed attention in recent years, and many modern liturgies have been written with his work as a guide. His book is a manual of church worship and discipline.

The Eucharist is described in two settings, the first after the consecration of a bishop and the second after a baptism. After the consecration, the bishop was given the "kiss of peace." Then the deacons brought the bread and wine (which was called an oblation). He and all the presbyters laid hands on the elements and then there was a dialogue with the congregation (*Sursum Corda*, "Lift up your hearts"):

Bishop: The Lord be with you.
People: And with thy spirit.
Bishop: Lift up your hearts.

People: We have them with the Lord.
Bishop: Let us give thanks unto the Lord.
People: It is meet and right.

Then followed the prayer that was eventually known as the *Canon* or the *Anaphora*. *Anaphora* is Greek and means "offer up." *Canon* comes from the Greek meaning "rule," and it was used as a title to indicate that the text from that point on was fixed.

But that was not the case with Hippolytus. He made it quite clear that the bishop was free to pray "according to his own ability." The prayer was a thanksgiving to God for creation by the Word, for the Incarnation of the Word, and for redemption through the suffering, death, and resurrection of the Word. That led to the words of institution and a prayer that the Holy Spirit would come upon the offering of the church and upon the partakers. The call for consecration (*Epiclesis*) would find an increasing place in subsequent liturgies. Then Hippolytus gave prayers to bless the offering of oil or cheese and olives. Offerings in the church were not perfunctory, nor were they minimized in the liturgy. People brought what they could to the Lord and it was joyfully gathered.

The second description of a Eucharist adds the interesting practice of having three cups, one of wine, one of milk and honey, and one of water. The instructions are not clear, but there was a partaking of each of the cups with the trinitarian formula, "In God the Father, Son, and Holy Spirit." The recipient said *Amen* after each.

Though forms were not fixed in great detail by that time, the expectation of what would be said and done was certainly more uniform. The approach to the Eucharist would include introductory dialogue, thanks to God for the work of Christ, the words of institution, *Anamnesis* (remembrance), *Epiclesis* (Holy Spirit to come), and doxology. Yet within that framework there was still a great deal of liberty.

Meanwhile, preaching and teaching based on the apostolic writings continued in force. There is a tendency to overlook that reality in the concentration upon certain theological developments in the first four centuries.

To compare the work of Justin Martyr and Hippolytus is to see the emergence of the twofold content of worship. The Liturgy of the Word included the opening salutation, the readings from Old and New Testaments, with the Psalms as response to the readings, and the sermon. The Liturgy of the Upper Room contained the offertory, which included the elements for communion, the *Sursum Corda* ("Lift up your hearts"), a consecration prayer, which included the *Sanctus* ("Holy, Holy, Holy Lord"), words of institution, *Anamnesis* (remembrance), *Epiclesis* (invocation of the Holy Spirit), intercessions, and the Lord's Prayer.

It is important for us to see not only the form the worship took, but also the purpose behind it. There were necessary and precious truths constantly re-presented by means of the worship. The person and work of Jesus Christ were central, and the fullness of His presence was ministered by Word and sacrament.

The Orthodox Church

The Orthodox church is important to us in understanding worship because worship is what it has majored in. In fact, *orthodox* means "right or true worship," or "right glory"—not merely right doctrine.

The Orthodox church broke with the West in the "Great Schism" in A.D. 1054. In that year the delegates from Rome were expelled from Constantinople, and the bishop of Rome's name was removed from the remembrance tables at the altar. Actually, the schism had begun much earlier, in the ninth century, and did not take place at a precise moment. After the official break, however, the patriarchs of the East continued in their places, with equal claim to apostolic succession, and never acknowledged the primacy of the pope of Rome. The true succession of the Orthodox church has never been questioned by the West. It is hard for many today to understand the great passion that in early times could be aroused by various ideas and liturgical practices.

For the Orthodox Christian, the "divine liturgy" is the focus and center of all Christian life. That liturgy is preserved in essentially the same form in which it has been observed for at least a thousand years. I will resist the temptation to point out many interesting aspects of Orthodox life and teaching. The worship is our concern.

The Orthodox church kept and developed the liturgies of the ancient church. The one service most frequently used is called the Liturgy of St. John Chrysostom. Much of its material is both earlier and later than Chrysostom (c. A.D. 400), but it is all obviously ancient, and there is no concern in the Orthodox church that it be modified or reformed. That is because for them worship reflects the constant activity of heaven and the Church Triumphant. Therefore, the worship of the Church Militant is a participation in that higher worship. That means that today's congregation, physically gathered, will always be vastly outnumbered by the myriads of saints and angels who will be there carrying on their perpetual adoration of God.

The New Testament foundation here is, of course, Hebrews 12:22–24:

But you have come to Mount Zion and to the city of the living God, the heavenly Jerusalem, and to innumerable angels in festal gathering, and to the assembly of the first-born who are enrolled in heaven, and to a judge who is God of all, and to the spirits of just men made perfect, and to Jesus, the mediator of a new covenant, and to the sprinkled blood that speaks more graciously than the blood of Abel.

That principle influences several aspects of Orthodox worship. It means that the church is unashamedly to be given a decor that reminds the congregation of heaven. And if we who worship Christ are "in the heavenlies," the worship is heavenly. Therefore, the most elaborate and costly decoration is eminently appropriate. That also means that sacred reminders of the heavenly congregation are in order. The icons, elaborately decorated pictures of the saints, apostles, the Virgin Mary, Christ, and Old Testament worthies, are very strange to Western eyes. To obey the biblical injunction against "graven images," any flesh of the person is painted on a flat surface. However, all other parts—clothing, scenery, halos—are often of exquisitely wrought silver, gold, or gems. All such items have elaborate regulations as to how they are to be made, and they are the sole province of religious orders rather than secular or commercial artists.

Many of the icons are placed in a screen in the church called the "iconostasis" that separates the sanctuary (where Christ is offered) from the congregation. There are three doors in the screen. The center, the Royal Door, leads to the altar and is opened only once during the service. The left-hand door is the "Little Entrance," used when the Gospel is brought out for reading. The right-hand door leads to a vestry where priest and bishop robe themselves.

The service is filled with symbolic actions, and the whole drama of redemption is depicted. It is lengthy and often repetitive. Perhaps a bare outline will give us a sense of the form of the service:

Liturgy of St. Chrysostom

Office of Preparation—of bread and wine. Priest behind screen.

Enarxis

Litany of *Pesach* (Great Litany)—a litany being a series of prayers by the priest with a formal response from the congregation, e.g., "Lord, have mercy."

Psalm 102 and the Little Litany

Psalm 145 and a hymn

The Little Litany

The Beatitudes

Liturgy of the Word

The Little Entrance and hymn

Trisagion—(Holy God, Holy and Strong, Holy and Immortal)

Prokeimenon—Verses, usually from Psalms

The Epistle, then Alleluia sung nine times

The Gospel

The Sermon or Homily

Intercession for the Church

Three Litanies

The Eucharist

Two short Litanies

The Great Entrance—(Bread and Wine to Holy Table)

The Peace and a cry, "The Doors," a remembrance of dismissal of catechumens (though misplaced)

Nicene Creed

Eucharistic Prayer

Preface

Canon

Institution

Anamnesis

Epiclesis

Commemoration of Mary, saints, living and departed

Doxology
Litany of Supplication and Lord's Prayer
Communion
Thanksgiving
Blessing

Distribution of *Antidoron* (Unconsecrated bread given to visitors and non-communicants)

In most Orthodox churches there are no seats, except around the wall. People often come and go, assume any posture they wish and move about rather freely. Communion is administered by a spoon from the cup into which the consecrated portion of the bread has been placed.

In America especially, the significance of this large body of Christians and the tradition of worship it has preserved is largely lost. Its churches are few and nearly always predominantly ethnic. Liturgies that are elaborate, lengthy, and performed in a foreign language are not particularly inviting. Yet any Christian should be aware of the history and practice of some 100 million people worldwide who gather in the name of Christ and seek to worship and live in a way that honors Him.

It is obvious that the Orthodox church has retained a glorious sense of mystery and awe in worship. Yet it has also emphasized the resurrection and ascension of Christ and has brought them into the Eucharist in a way not matched in the West. There are biblical and patristic prayers and a skillful use of devout silence. The attitude of worship is carried into common life, largely through the use of prayers and the sign of the cross in a multitude of situations. There are actually prayers devised for almost every activity of life. An Orthodox Christian would perhaps cross himself at the beginning of a bus ride (and well he might in many places in the world).

In some ways the Eastern church has avoided some of

the problems of the West. Orthodox priests (but not bishops) marry, although they cannot remarry. The Orthodox church has always put its liturgy into the language of the people. It has a high view of Christ present in the Eucharist, and it has refused any philosophical or scientific exploration as to how the mystery occurs. It has not experienced schism, and it has managed to survive in a variety of political environments. It still calls faithful Christian people to worship, and they come with a commitment that is challenging and persistent.

STUDY GUIDE

1. What do you find surprising or unusual in the worship instructions of the *Didache*?
2. We found some liturgical terms that are important: *Anaphora, Canon, Anamnesis, Epiclesis*. They were and are a part of the Eucharist. Describe them.
3. Some of your group may have attended a Greek or Eastern Orthodox church. You might wish to do so if there is one in your community. Usually, just the sight of the interior of the church will be well-remembered. An Orthodox priest or deacon could be invited to explain their worship.
4. Many of the Protestant objections to Roman Catholic practices do not apply to the Orthodox. Can you identify some of those?

7

Worship in the Medieval and Roman Catholic Church

No Christian today can fully understand the theology and tradition of worship without a serious look at the medieval church. There one sees an amazing period of growth and change that stretched over 1000 years and more. When we remember that the Protestant Reformation took place only 450 years ago, we can begin to appreciate the significance of the huge segment of Christian history that came before it. It should be obvious to us all that there were a great many magnificent Christian leaders, bishops, theologians, abbots, priests, saints, and martyrs who are properly claimed by every Christian as spiritual forebears. Their loyalty to the bishop of Rome, along with their loyalty to their own bishops and leaders, is something we respect.

But our purpose is to trace the development of the dialogue of worship to discover how it emerged from that long period and what contributions have been made to us now. Getting a handle on fifteen hundred years of history is no easy task, but we will try to summarize and crystallize while still doing justice to the material.

1. Change in Civil/Church Status

In A.D. 313, the Emperor Constantine issued the Edict of Toleration, and the Christian church was launched into an entirely new era. We still feel the results of his action. It is very hard for us to imagine what it would be like to be a part of a church that had been persecuted and generally abused and misunderstood for two hundred years, then all of a sudden able to boast of the emperor as one of its flock.

Almost overnight the church had changed from being a minority of slaves and peasants to being a company of citizens with full rights, whose leaders were now given the same honor and recognition as other dignitaries, both religious and civil. Most of us would have reacted pretty much as those Christians of the fourth century. Bishops and presbyters were given the trappings of leadership that they had not had before. It is no wonder that the beginning of the separation of clergy and laity can be marked at that point, to proceed almost unabated to the present time. That is not to say it would not have occurred otherwise, but its ultimate effect on the act of worship is unquestionable. Worship would become more and more the province of the leader rather than the encounter with God by the people.

2. The Change in Language

Until Constantine's time, the language of the Roman Empire, especially in intellectual and cultural matters, had been largely Greek. Our friend Hippolytus wrote in Greek, although a copy in the original language has been lost to us. Now began the shift to Latin, which we know became the liturgical language that dominated the Roman Catholic church until 1963. Again the dialogue of worship was affected. There might be a kind of uniformity that is gratifying in a worldwide liturgical language, but the price in the loss of a truly participating congregation is enormous.

3. The Development of the Mass

The "Mass" is virtually synonymous in the minds of many Christians with the Roman Catholic church. It certainly has been the great focus of meaning and devotion for the Roman Catholic parishioner. As we have already noted, many trace the origin of the word to the Latin word *missa*, which was part of the closing sentence of the Latin service. The important thing for us to realize is that the Mass was a continuation of the synagogue service of the Word and the Christian observance of the Lord's Supper—Word and sacrament. That basic form of Christian worship offers no problem to most Christians, but obviously the development of the Mass introduced matters that seriously divided the church and tended to obscure the dialogue of worship. What follows is a discussion of some developments that have caused problems for the worship of the church.

Uniformity. There is always a kind of built-in tendency for sameness in the development of worship forms. Although that is not necessarily bad, it can eventually result in deadening formalism, which certainly happened to the dialogue of worship in the Middle Ages. Two of the most influential leaders in the development were the two Gregorys: Gregory (I) the Great, who was pope from A.D. 590 to 604; and Gregory VII (Hildebrand), who held office from 1073 to 1085.

To some extent, the reforms were practical and called for. Gregory I noted that some papal masses were three hours in length! That was a bit much, even for popes. He put together four different volumes for guidance in the liturgy, covering such matters as prayers for the Eucharist for the entire liturgical year, music for the choir, a lectionary of the four Gospels, which is simply an arrangement of readings for the worship services, and a set of directions for the clergy regarding each ritual procedure. Those writings exerted great influence on the worship of the church for centuries.

Gregory VII's reign marked the beginning of the period

of the greatest power of the Roman church. One of the areas of his interest was the worship of the church, and he brought back to Rome both the authority and the concern about the structure of the Mass that had been lacking.

It should be recognized that some of the drive for uniformity arises from very admirable theological concerns. One of the ongoing struggles of the medieval church centered around the Arian heresy, which began with the teaching of Arius in the beginning of the fourth century. He felt that the absolute supremacy of God the Father demanded that Christ the Son be a created being and, therefore, properly less than true God. That idea, of course, was not acceptable to most theologians in the church, and it was formally refuted at the Council of Nicea in 325. The Nicene Creed formalized the doctrine of Christ's full deity and oneness with God the Father, a doctrine later set in concrete by the Council of Chalcedon and other pronouncements of the church. However, the heresy did not die, and large segments of the church, especially in missionary activity throughout Europe, were more or less affected by that view.

To combat the heresy, and for other pious reasons, statements about Christ in the Mass tended to place Him with the Father as the object of Christian devotion and prayer, rather than as mediator on our behalf for our adoration of the Father. Thus, we see again the amazing interplay of worship and theology, each constantly affecting the other.

Roman theologians and historians will agree that the Council of Trent culminated the drive for uniformity in worship and in almost all other aspects of the church. In 1563, at the twenty-fifth session of the Council, the task was given to the pope and his curia to produce a single Roman Catholic worship form. That move especially contributed to the end of any independence for the bishops. In 1568 an official book was published to regulate all that was done in the services of daily devotion—the "hours." In 1570 the *Missal Romanum* gave the worship service for every church that did not have a liturgy of its own dating back at least two hundred years. Now a priest or monk could celebrate the Mass with a single book, indeed, *should* celebrate the Mass as specified.

Domination of the Mass by the clergy. This development fed on itself, in that the more the Mass was removed from the participation of the worshiper, the freer the clergy became to control the structure and function of the Mass, which removed it even further. That led to such items as "secret" prayers, which were completely unknown to the congregation. The process was further aided when the Mass became the daily duty and obligation of the priest, rather than his participation with the people. It was a short step to "private" masses, said for someone living or dead, with no participating congregation whatever.

A side effect, as the Latin service became more and more distant from the congregation, was the proliferation of various other forms of piety, especially through the honoring of Mary. A believing and devoted Roman Catholic would often find outlet for profound spiritual dedication not through the weekly Mass, but through an alternative and more demanding exercise. After all, his attention was not asked other than at three points in the service—the offertory, the consecration, and the communion. The Mass itself tended toward more and more obscure allegory. The priest was acting out the drama of redemption, and everything meant something that he alone might know. For instance, the triple silence during the Mass—one at the secret prayer, one during the *Canon* (the fixed Eucharistic prayer), and one after the Lord's Prayer—represented the three days in the tomb. The five turns of the celebrant to the people were the five appearances of Christ after the resurrection. Such things—and there were many more—soon were lost to anyone but the celebrant.

The table, which in the earlier Roman churches had been in the center of a gathered congregation, was eventually moved to the east wall, and the celebrant had his back to the people much of the time. There was no need for an offertory procession, especially if the private Mass had already received the "Mass stipend." The practice of genuflection—bending the knee as an act of respect—became more indiscriminately used. Preaching continued to decline, although the church did not lack for some good preachers who were eagerly heard.

The sanctity and supremacy of the sacrament. Although the Eastern church had accepted the reality of the presence of the body of Christ in the Eucharist, it had resisted attempts to explain how the miracle occurred. The Western church, following Augustine, had regarded the presence of Christ as a spiritual reality. But from the seventh and eighth centuries on, there was an ever-increasing body of teaching that demanded the physical presence of the body and blood of Christ in the Eucharist. That idea is known as the doctrine of transubstantiation, and the most careful presentation of it is by the great medieval theologian, Thomas Aquinas (1225–1274). There has probably not been a person of greater intellect or greater devotion to Christ than the "Angelic Doctor." He formulated with great care a way by which the presence of Christ in the Eucharist could be understood in terms of the prevailing philosophy of his time, that of Aristotle.

Some of us will be aware of Aquinas's work, but briefly stated, his view was that the body and blood of Christ becomes the "substance" of bread and wine, even though their outward appearance, "accidents," retain their natural form and quality. Bread and wine still look and taste like bread and wine, but the inner reality, the "breadness," which that particular piece of bread somehow shares with all bread is replaced by the reality, the substance of the body of Christ. We must not forget that this was a pious and ingenious definition that was seen as a proper defense of a doctrine that might, without such definition, be a scandal. Aquinas and the Roman church were willing to accept the theological and practical implications of the doctrine in order to preserve the central reality of the presence of Christ with His people.

It is interesting to observe that most of the controversial teachings of the Roman Catholics have been "defensive" in character. Transubstantiation is an attempt to preserve rationally the real presence of Christ in the Eucharist; the cult of Mary, with its Immaculate Conception, Perpetual Virginity, and Bodily Assumption of the Virgin Mary, is an attempt to preserve the full yet sinless humanity of Jesus as well as His deity; the primacy of Peter and the papacy is an attempt to protect a high doctrine of the church. The list could continue.

But we are thinking of the effect on worship of that particular view of the Eucharist. Aquinas's definition eventually led to the withholding of the cup of wine from the laity. That was (and is) theologically justified by the assumption that Christ was indeed fully present in His body, which the bread became, so that the receiving worshiper truly partook of Christ. From a practical standpoint, there was less possibility of difficulty if the cup was withheld, since bread was much easier to handle than wine. Crumbs could be recovered, but what would one do about the "blood of Christ" spilled on the floor or on a garment? The priest, however, always received communion in both kinds, and the imbalance of the dialogue became more pronounced than ever.

There were numbers of attempts at reform from within the church, which finally bore fruit in Vatican II in the twentieth century. Yet the effect of Trent and the four hundred years of uniform and rigidly controlled worship practice in the Roman church was to produce a liturgy that had, in many ways, lost touch with the people.

Generalizations about and summaries of long periods of history are always dangerous, and one should not forget the magnificent contributions of the Roman church during the period we have surveyed. An illustration would be the work of Ambrose, bishop of Milan (A.D. 340–397). He was a poet and musician as well as a theologian-preacher. His creative gifts were expressed in hymn writing, and the words of "O Splendor of God's Glory Bright" and "O Jesus, Lord of Heavenly Grace" are in many of our hymnals. He probably had some part in the *Te Deum Laudamus* ("We Praise Thee, O God, we acknowledge Thee to be the Lord"). That prayer has been used extensively in more liturgical churches.

Thus began a tradition of worship music that affects the church to this day. Another contributor was Gregory the Great, whose name was attached to the music he sponsored, Gregorian chant. The name is often given to any kind of plain chant or song. The chant was unaccompanied, for the medieval church rejected musical instruments as pagan. Gregorian chant was the music of all churches, except those using the liturgy and hymns of Ambrose, until the fourteenth century when polyphonic music began its rise (music that used a chromatic scale and harmony). Interest in Gregorian chant was revived in the nineteenth century under the guidance of the Benedictines at Solesmes in France, and it was placed in official favor by Pius X in 1903. Chant does not follow the rhythmical pattern that we use in most choral music, but usually gives about equal time to each syllable. It can serve to make a text clearly understood when it is done properly, and the solemn beauty of its cadences, especially in a resonant cathedral, never fails to impress the hearer with its reverence and dignity.

The major contribution of the thousand years of Roman Catholic worship was the preservation of the shape or form of the liturgy. There were variations to be sure, but the Mass was a faithful continuation of the essentials of worship that the early church had found meaningful and essential.

4. The Christian Year

Another significant contribution to emerge from the medieval period was the development of the Christian or Church Year. It provided a pattern for worship that included the use of the Lectionary—a selection of Scripture passages for the liturgy. In its early and more simple form, the Church Year was the remembrance of the major events of the life of our Lord and also the coming of the Holy Spirit. As early as the fourth century, the Christians in Jerusalem were doing special things on the occasions of Passover and Pentecost, the time of the Crucifixion, the Resurrection, and the advent of the Holy Spirit. That practice made a natural bridge from Judaism to Christianity, but it also intensified the significance of those precious events. Over the years the basic format was expanded both in the East and in the West to include other events in the life and ministry of our Lord and the division of the year into "seasons."

The beginning of the Church Year is the season of Advent, including the four Sundays prior to Christmas that are observed as a time of penitence and preparation. Advent is not only for remembering Christ's birth, but also for remembering His Second Coming in power and glory, for which we must all indeed prepare.

Christmas finally became a separate season, although it was originally a part of Epiphany, which means "manifestation." Epiphany was set on January 6 (the twelfth day of Christmas) and is used to remember both the baptism of Jesus and His manifestation to the world, as symbolized by the coming of the Magi or Wise Men.

Lent is the forty-day period of preparation for Easter and, more especially, the preparation for baptism of new converts to Christianity. Lent begins on Ash Wednesday, a time of confession and penitence. Holy Week begins with the Triumphal Entry of our Lord on Palm Sunday and goes on to Maundy Thursday, Good Friday, and Easter.

Ascension Day and Pentecost (forty days and seven Sundays after Easter) are followed by six months during which the doctrines of the New Testament regarding the church and its life in the world are to be examined. This is the season of the church on earth, the Church Militant.

All intervening Sundays during that time had their proper Scripture lessons (from the Lectionary), which were observed in order to preserve for the church the regular and deliberate consideration of the central realities of Christ and the gospel. The Roman church, however, allowed the calendar to become jammed with observances for the saints, and often the benefits of the gospel were overshadowed by the sheer weight of the saints' days.

More and more churches, including many evangelical ones, have seen the benefit of such an orderly approach to worship and are following a Church Year calendar of some form or other.

5. Vatican II to the Present

It is very difficult for those of us outside the Roman church to understand the full impact upon the church of the Second Vatican Council. There was no area of the Roman church left untouched, and no greater reforms took place than in the worship of the faithful.

Pope John XXIII surprised the world with his call for a Second Vatican Council and the *Aggorniamento*, the refurbishing of Catholic life. He wanted the windows opened and fresh breezes to blow. For some church leaders it seemed a hurricane. The Council met and established on 4

December 1963, four hundred years to the day after the similar act of the Council of Trent, the Constitution on the Sacred Liturgy. It is an impressive document and its implications are still being worked out in the church today.

What has happened to worship and liturgy in the Roman church as a result? First, a theology of liturgy has been restated that seeks to place worship at the center of the life of the church. Worship is defined in terms of the "Paschal mystery," which is focused on the Eucharist, but which is adequately understood and celebrated by all the people of God—clergy and laity—in their proper roles.

Such celebration must also include all the ways by which the "Paschal mystery" is understood and mediated. That includes the reading and preaching of the Word of God, especially the gospel, which is interpreted as pointing toward some aspect of the Paschal mystery that is resident in the central reality of Christ, crucified and risen. Humankind is saved through the blood of Christ, and the church is to announce that redemptive work in her worship and is constantly to expose its richness and sufficiency. In that action it joins together with its Risen Head to fellowship in a renewed sacrificial meal, "until He comes."

Second, the restatement of the purpose and meaning of the liturgy naturally results in its reform. If the parishioners are to make their contribution to the liturgy, then it must be suited to their understanding and comprehension. It must, therefore, be adapted properly to different groups in all its aspects. Bishops, priests, deacons, and parishioners must all be in their proper place and carry out their proper function so that the Paschal mystery may be fully demonstrated.

One result of that understanding is that the liturgy demands a living language. Liturgical Latin was thus discouraged, and bishops were instructed to provide their flocks with a liturgy in the language of the people. That change alone has reverberated through the Roman Catholic church and served to open the liturgy to comprehension and participation by millions.

The structure of a Liturgy of the Word and a Liturgy of the Upper Room has demanded a restoration of preaching. Every Sunday Mass must have a sermon. It may be brief according to evangelical standards, but it is a sermon, where before there might have been a few parish announcements or nothing at all.

Third, the placing of responsibility for worship in the hands of bishops has been part of the tendency to acknowledge diversity within unity as normative for Catholic worship. Varying traditions have been recognized, and the way has been opened for different cultures to bring their own resources to enrich the act of worship. That variety has even allowed the emergence of charismatic worship (which we will discuss later), with the approval of some bishops. There has been a veritable flood of new music for the Mass and the same rash of experimentation that characterized much Protestant worship in the 1960s and 1970s.

There is still the possibility of very traditional worship in the Roman church, but a visit by a Protestant to a Catholic church will reveal much that is immediately recognized and appreciated. It is still forbidden by the church to administer the Eucharist to a non-Catholic (that is, to someone who does not share the Roman understanding of the significance of the bread and wine). However, the means of enforcing that rule are not stringent. There are isolated cases of concelebration (two or more priests or ministers celebrating the Eucharist together), and the communion is now given in both kinds (bread and wine) in marriage Eucharists and certain other occasions.

Each Sunday, the average Roman Catholic worshiper uses a "Missalette," a leaflet that prints the order of the Mass and the various parts that change each week. Those changes (known as Propers) are the only thing that would give a non-Catholic any problem. The Propers are printed together. For instance, the Old Testament lessons for each Sunday in the month are all on one page, and you would read only the one for a particular Sunday and then skip over to the next part of the Mass. This is an outline of the normal Sunday Mass today:

Introductory Rites
    Entrance Song—Celebrant and ministers go to the altar
    Greeting
    Penitential Rite
        Confession and Absolution
        Kyrie (*Kyrie eleison*—Greek for "Lord, have mercy")
        Gloria
        Opening Prayer—One of the Propers

Liturgy of the Word
    First Reading—Old Testament
        Responsorial Psalm
    Second Reading—Epistle
        Alleluia or Acclamation
    Gospel
    Homily
    Creed
    Prayer of the Faithful—Varied prayers with response

Liturgy of the Eucharist
    Preparation of the Gifts
    Prayer over the Gifts—Proper of the Mass
    Eucharistic Prayer
        Preface—Proper
        Sanctus and Benedictus
        Eucharistic Prayer I (*Canon*)
        Memorial Acclamation of the People
        Memorial Prayer

Rite of Communion
  Lord's Prayer
  Peace
  Agnus Dei (Commingling and communion of the priest)
  Communion Song—Proper or a hymn
  People's communion
  Prayer after communion—Proper

Concluding Rite
  Greeting and Blessing
  Dismissal

Other than the readings and psalm, each part is usually only a few lines long, and a Mass is normally about an hour, including a ten-minute homily.

The centrality of the Mass in the Roman church is unquestionable. Millions of people around the world find it personally and corporately rewarding. All Christians can learn something to enrich their own understanding of worship from it. When it was stripped of its Latin obscurity, it was discovered to be a collection of Scripture, prayer, sermon, creed, and ceremony that is at the root of our common Christian heritage.

STUDY GUIDE

1. It is very possible that you have had occasion to attend Roman Catholic worship. Perhaps you can go again and recognize the parts of the service with greater insight. There are many "styles" of worship in the Roman church and your group may have experienced them. A Roman priest would certainly visit your

group if asked. Any Roman Catholic church would be happy to give you some Missalettes for your study. What aspect of Roman worship impresses you as most helpful?

2. See if you can discover a hymn in your hymnal by Ambrose of Milan. You might also be interested in finding the words of the *Te Deum*.

3. Gregorian chant has received a good deal of attention from some church musicians. Recordings are available. Buy one, or borrow one from your local library, listen to it, and discuss your impressions with the group.

4. Notice carefully the actions of Vatican II. What is "different" about Roman Catholic worship now from pre-Vatican II practices?

5. What is the value of the Christian Year for worship?

6. What are pros and cons of using a Lectionary?

8

Traditional Worship:
Lutheran and Anglican (Episcopal)

Now we are ready to move to the fascinating task of discovering just how our contemporary traditions of Protestant worship were developed. You may be familiar with some of them. Perhaps you have visited different churches and observed the varied forms of worship.

Remember that the quality of worship leadership in various churches differs widely. In all denominations and groups there are churches that strive for excellence, usually led by competent and dedicated people. There are also churches that fall far short in that regard. I am hoping that your study of the various traditions, including your own, will enable you to maximize your joy and gratification in your worship participation.

The Protestant Reformation is capable of analysis from several significant viewpoints—theological, political, economic, ecclesiastical, and liturgical. Our purpose is to look at the effects of the Reformation on the worship of the church so that we can understand the various traditions of worship that are with us in Protestant worship today. There is no question that when we see with clarity the process by which worship has come to be expressed in various ways, we will become better participants in our particular tradition. It is hoped we can look honestly and openly at those developments in order to recognize their validity and meaning.

There is a slogan that is ancient with theologians: *lex orandi est lex credendi*, "the law of prayer is the law of faith" (what is believed). That is to say that the church at worship is the place where its theology and teaching are born, and not vice versa. We have already alluded to that idea, but perhaps it will be reinforced as we look at the patterns of worship emerging from the Reformation. The Reformation is complex, and this is a point in that complexity.

Is the Reformation, then, a change that began in worship and spread into theology? It isn't that simple. Over a long period of time there was a theology that built itself on the liturgy. Sacrament triumphed over the Word, and a theology was developed to explain and justify it. The reformers rejected that theology in varying degrees, and the way in which they reformed the theology is clearly seen in what they did in worship.

The place where the Reformation made the greatest impact was not in theology but in the liturgy! For the average person in the mid-1500s, theology was secondary to worship. It was in worship he could recognize change and discover its meaning and purpose.

1. Lutheran Worship

For most of us, the Reformation *is* Martin Luther. We may not be Lutheran, but we give common acknowledgement as Christians to the monk of Wittenburg who was the instrument of such monumental change. We will not review the history except to place in context what problems and solutions in worship Luther engineered.

Every aspect of the Reformation is shot through with the radical rediscovery of the Word of God. The reformers sought to follow and honor that rediscovery in every aspect of church life. Amazingly enough, when it came to worship, Luther was perfectly willing to retain existing forms in the Mass as long as nothing was forbidden by Scripture. He clearly saw how sensitive the worshiper was to changes in liturgy, and he was much more conservative about that than many who surrounded him.

For Luther, the Scripture was a criterion but not a source for the construction of liturgy. In 1523, he published the *Formulae Missae,* the formula for the Mass. It was in Latin, and it actually contained most of the Roman rite. The changes are both expected and puzzling. He was consistently concerned about the place given the Word and preaching: "When God's Word is not preached, it would be better that no one should sing, read or come together." As late as 1544 he wrote describing an "evangelical service . . . that we may come together to act and to hear God's Word . . . that our dear Lord Himself may speak to us through His holy Word . . . that we in our turn may speak to Him through prayer and songs of praise."[1] The preaching and hearing of the Word were at the heart of worship.

Most of the "Mass of the Catechumens" (Liturgy of the Word), therefore, survived intact, although he thought of putting the sermon in a more dramatic place than after the creed. But he did not leave the Mass of the Faithful (Liturgy of the Eucharist) alone. He removed the Offertory since it was the introduction to a kind of sacrificial action that he repudiated. He wanted the Eucharist understood as a *beneficium,* not a *sacrificium.* Luther felt that doctrine had opened the door to Roman abuses, including all the votive Masses and private Masses. The Eucharist is not a sacrifice offered by men to God, but a gracious gift of God to man.

The service then proceeded to the *Sursum Corda* ("Lift up your hearts") and a short preface that led to the Words of Institution. He put the *Sanctus* ("Holy, Holy") and the *Benedictus* ("Blessed is He that cometh") after the consecration prayer. Then the Lord's Prayer and the "Peace" were followed by the communion, again using Roman words. The *Agnus Dei* and German hymns were sung while the people communed. The service closed with the traditional blessing.

Luther used vernacular hymns in the 1523 service and predicted the necessity of an entire service in the vernacular. That was quickly forthcoming. In 1526 he published the *Deutsche Messe* (German Mass). He really envisioned three services to be used by the church. He wanted the Latin service (1523) so that youth could be trained in more than one language. He wished they could sing, read, and hold Mass in Greek and Hebrew as well! He wanted the German service for the laity, and he especially wanted to have good order in presenting the gospel to those who were not yet Christians. The third service would be a special gathering, probably in a home, for those who were truly serious about their Christianity. They would be enrolled, perform the sacraments, and take care of each other. He admitted not having any candidates for that type of worship.

Luther made some significant contributions to the development of worship. The Bible, hymns, prayers, and the entire service in the language of the people were the greatest contributions. Luther himself wrote thirty-seven hymns and began a tradition in the church that has enriched us all. *Ein Feste Burg* ("A Mighty Fortress") is in all hymnals and has recently appeared in Missalettes and other service music in the Roman Catholic church! The musical tradition begun by Luther includes such great composers as J. S. Bach, and it has left us a heritage that is rich and grand.

Luther, as with most of the reformers, attempted to preserve the unity of Word and sacrament in worship. He also gave back the communion to the people in both kinds, bread and wine. But Luther's conservatism is certainly demonstrated in his teaching about the Eucharist. His demand that the elements be recognized as both Body and bread, both Blood and wine, was not a radical departure from Rome. He refused to allow the idea of a physical change of bread into Body, but he wanted to preserve the literal integrity of Jesus' words, "This is my body." His confrontation with Zwingli at Marburg, where he wrote with chalk on the table, *Hoc est corpus meum* ("This is my body"), is one of the classic moments of the Reformation. That doctrine of Luther's is known as "consubstantiation," in contrast to the Roman "transubstantiation."

It is important for us to observe that the statements of those doctrines are not mutually exclusive, but the effect on liturgy and worship is profound. It was what had been allowed to happen when the Roman church worshiped that Luther found offensive. He traced correctly to the theology behind it, and in mild and then more significant ways changed the worship to express that revision. But the Lutheran tradition is essentially a conservative one as far as worship is concerned.

In Europe, in the centuries since the Reformation, Lutheranism has witnessed a deterioration of sacramental life. As in other Protestant churches, the Liturgy of the Word became the major service. Tragically, both the Eucharist and the daily offices (devotional services of prayer and reading) declined. That, of course, has been reflected in the American scene, which is why so much of modern Protestantism, though proficient in Bible teaching, is virtually starving to death for true worship.

There have been three large bodies of Lutherans in the United States—the Lutheran Church in America (LCA), the American Lutheran Church (ALC), and the Lutheran Church—Missouri Synod. The first two, along with a smaller synod, have recently merged to form one Lutheran denomination. There are also some smaller Lutheran groups, including the Church of the Lutheran Brethren, the Lutheran Church—Wisconsin Synod, and others. There is naturally some variety in their worship, yet a common tradition underlies them all.

Some significant work that affects most Lutheran

churches has been done since the formation in 1966 of the Inter-Lutheran Commission on Worship. The three largest Lutheran groups were joined by the Evangelical Lutheran Church of Canada. In 1969 the Commission published Contemporary Worship 1: Hymns (CW 1). Similar work followed with publication of Services for Holy Communion (CW 2), Marriage (CW 3), Service of the Word (CW 5), the Church Year, Calendar, and Lectionary (CW 6), Holy Baptism (CW 7), and the Affirmation of the Baptismal Covenant (CW 8). The Lectionary followed the new Roman Catholic lectionary, a three-year cycle. The service of baptismal affirmation is the revision of confirmation and first communion, an attempt to restructure confirmation to be a part of the sacrament of baptism rather than being understood as a separate action.

The final work in the series was the 1978 publication of the *Lutheran Book of Worship*. Some of its objectives are:

> to continue to move into the larger ecumenical heritage of liturgy while, at the same time, enhancing Lutheran convictions about the Gospel; to involve lay persons as assisting ministers who share the leadership of corporate worship; to bring the language of prayer and praise into conformity with the best current usage; to offer a variety of musical styles. (p. 8)

The book provides all necessary service material for the liturgical life of the church, including hymns. There are collects, readings, prayers, three settings for communion, baptism, a service of the Word, morning and evening prayer, readings for daily prayer, corporate and individual confession, marriage, and a burial service. The first setting for Holy Communion is:

Entrance Hymn
Greeting
Kyrie
Hymn of Praise—Gloria or other hymn
Collect

First Lesson
Psalm
Second Lesson
Versicle (Alleluia)
Gospel

Sermon

Hymn of the Day
Nicene (or Apostles') Creed

Prayers
Passing of the Peace
Offering
Great Thanksgiving
Lord's Prayer
Communion
Post-Communion hymn and prayer
Blessing

Dismissal

There is provision for a service without communion that continues from the creed. Confession and absolution may occur before the entrance hymn or at the offertory. The absolution continues Luther's insistence that properly ordained ministers pronounce absolution. The minister says, "As a called and ordained minister of the Church of Christ and by his authority, I therefore declare to you the entire forgiveness of all your sins, in the name of the Father, and of the Son, and of the Holy Spirit."

The book of worship is an excellent preservation of Lutheran tradition that in general form retains the shape of the Mass. The worship of the Lutheran church reflects that commitment to historical tradition along with a desire for evangelical vitality.

2. Anglican Worship: The Church of England and the Episcopal Church in America

We have placed the Episcopal church with the Lutheran as a church of "traditional" worship. That is not so much a theological as a liturgical classification. The Anglican church still makes some claim not to be a Protestant church, even though it was titled until recently the Protestant Episcopal Church in the United States of America. That claim enables it to maintain continuity as one "catholic and apostolic church," even though neither the Roman nor Orthodox church has acknowledged its apostolic succession.

The complexity of history that revolves around Henry VIII and his relationship to the pope is not part of our present consideration. Some of the history, however, involves part of the development of worship and liturgy in England, which in turn has had profound influence on the worship practices of the English-speaking world. The changes in the worship of the church in England in the middle of the sixteenth century were in many ways a modification of Roman practice. They, like the Lutheran reforms, were not all that radical. But once changed, the church formed a tradition that has persevered into the twentieth century.

The focus of the tradition for the Episcopal church is the Book of Common Prayer. There is no question that this collection of rites and ceremonies has been, along with preservation of the episcopal system of church government, the major contribution of the Anglican church to the religious world.

The influence of the Prayer Book on virtually all the traditions in the English-speaking world is enormous. If not felt directly in the Sunday service, it is evidenced in many churches in the marriages, funerals, baptisms, and often the Eucharist, which are filled with phrases or whole sections from the Book of Common Prayer.

The man who put that book together was Thomas Cranmer. Like the other influential persons of the sixteenth century, he was a remarkable combination of intelligence and devotion. He served as archbishop of Canterbury from 1532 until he was executed as a heretic under the Roman Catholic reign of Mary in 1556. He was cautious to the point of inconsistency, although few of us can appreciate the problems of threading one's way successfully through the intrigues and complexities of church and state in the time of Henry VIII. And it is also to be remembered that he died for his convictions, even though he at first recanted. We cannot take the space to look at the process in detail, but it is important that we see Cranmer's work as a gradual reformation of liturgy in much the same fashion as Luther's.

The force behind that gradualism was the profound desire for unity. On the one side, Henry VIII wanted his kingdom to hold together, and on the other side Cranmer and his contemporaries sincerely wanted the church reformed, but with a national unity that would prove healthy and constructive. Anglicanism was a gigantic effort to produce a truly national church in which the sovereign assumed a proper role as defender and titular head along with the bishops, priests, and deacons, who also carried responsibility for the body politic.

The first thing that was done was to introduce the English Bible into every church and to have it read in the Sunday services (1547). Some have tried to say that Henry VIII wanted prayers in the churches in English so that people would pray for his success in battle. Although that may be true, King Henry was very aware of the theological and ec-clesiastical issues at hand.

There is no question about the theological and liturgical sources of Cranmer's work. The dominant liturgy in En-gland had come to be the Sarum rite, which was centered in the historic cathedral at Salisbury. Cranmer also used the work of some foreign church leaders. One was a Span-ish cardinal named Quignonez who had published a book of the divine office, the daily devotions of the church. An-other was a work of the bishop of Cologne, Nicholas von Wied, called *Consultations*.

England had also been visited by some of the reformers from Geneva. Cranmer was a student of both Zwingli and Luther, so the combination of Reformation influences was sizeable.

Cranmer produced in 1549 a prayer book that attempted and accomplished some amazing tasks. It adopted two of the offices observed by monasteries and churches as the major expressions of worship. Those were simply termed morning and evening prayer. In the more ancient form, they had been matins and vespers. We will review later the development of those offices, but the appropriateness for the average person of morning and evening prayer can hardly be missed. They were to be read daily by priests, and the people as well, if at all possible.

Cranmer also devised a service for the Eucharist. There were still a large number of English people who were loyal to the Roman doctrines, including a bishop named Gar-diner. Cranmer had in mind a service that would be true to Reformation principles (here Zwingli seems to have been very influential) and yet give as little offense to the Roman-ists as possible. He carefully avoided any statement that would make the Mass a sacrifice, but he did not avoid ter-minology which made the bread and wine *to the receiver* the Body and Blood of Christ. For instance, the Eucharistic Prayer states,

And here we offer Thee ourselves, our souls and bodies, to be a living sacrifice ... having in remembrance his blessed passion and precious death, his mighty resurrection and glorious ascension, rendering unto Thee most hearty thanks for the innumerable benefits procured unto us by the same.

And in the prayer of consecration,

... vouchsafe to bless and sanctify, with thy Word and Holy Spirit, these thy gifts and creatures of bread and wine; that we, receiving them according to thy Son our Saviour Jesus Christ's holy institution, in remembrance of his death and passion, may be partakers of his most blessed Body and Blood.

The statement of the priest to the communicant was the following:

The Body of our Lord Jesus Christ, which was given for thee, preserve thy body and soul unto everlasting life. Take and eat this in remembrance that Christ died for thee, *and feed on him in thy heart by faith*, with thanksgiving.... Drink this in remembrance that Christ's Blood was shed for thee, and be thankful.

Note the "feed on him in thy heart," and "eat (drink) this in remembrance." Those are Reformation words, but possible in the context to be given almost any meaning one wishes.

Cranmer succeeded almost too well. Bishop Gardiner, though loyal to Rome, found the 1549 prayer book unoffensive. That fact was close to being the kiss of death, for there were many who called for clearer reformation. Although there was every intention to continue prayer book revision, Gardiner's reaction speeded the publication of a second book in 1552. That is not to say that Cranmer changed his views between the first and second book, or that the changes made were anything but what was originally foreseen. The new book proved to be more specifically Reformed and less Catholic, although still not absolutely either one.

Thus begins a bit of history that is interesting to an understanding of the American Episcopal church. The Anglican church in Scotland retained the 1549 Prayer Book, and in revolutionary times the Scottish church provided both bishops and Prayer Book for the American church.

The English world is fortunate that a man of Cranmer's gifts applied himself to liturgy. Though we are impressed with the Tudor English of Shakespeare and the King James Version of the Bible, not all Tudor English attains the intelligibility, the dignity, and the energy that Cranmer's does. He aimed at being biblical, clear, and edifying. His sense of phrasing and balance was magnificent. Consider the famous "Prayer of Humble Access":

> We do not presume to come to this thy Table, O merciful Lord, trusting in our own righteousness, but in thy manifold and great mercies. We are not worthy so much as to gather up the crumbs under thy Table. But thou art the same Lord, whose property is always to have mercy: Grant us therefore, gracious Lord, so to eat the flesh of thy dear Son Jesus Christ, and to drink his blood, that our sinful bodies may be made clean by his body, and our souls washed through his most precious blood, and that we may evermore dwell in him, and he in us. Amen.

The evangelical John Wesley paid tribute to Cranmer's work by incorporating it virtually untouched in the order for the Eucharist of the Methodist church.

What has happened to worship and liturgy in the Anglican and Episcopalian churches? There have been various revisions of the Book of Common Prayer. Puritan pressures resulted in the revision of 1662. Anglicanism moved out of England into the expanded British Empire, and the

Book of Common Prayer was translated and modified.

The move to America through the colonies had an interesting history. Though many of the colonists were Anglicans, the church suffered greatly for two reasons. For one thing, because of political pressure the bishops of England refused to ordain a bishop for the colonies, and as a result, ordinations and confirmations were difficult and long delayed. It was the Scottish church that finally provided a bishop for America. The other problem was the loyalty of many Anglican colonists to the bishop and king in England. The national church concept would reinforce such Tory loyalty, but once the revolution was over, the attitude of many Americans toward the Anglican loyalists would not be friendly. Many of the clergy had fled to Canada in a genuine confusion over the issues that the revolution posed.

In 1790 the first American Prayer Book was published. It was a cautious work, largely derived from the Scottish Prayer Book of 1764. It was revised in 1892 and 1928. In 1973 further revision was begun, and a book of services "for trial use" was published. It was utilized three years, and in 1976 the General Convention issued a "Proposed Book of Common Prayer" as an authorized alternative for three years. In 1979 the "proposed" book was officially adopted by the General Convention and it is now the Service Book for the Episcopal Church in the United States.

The new Prayer Book makes possible the daily offices of morning and evening prayer and the service of the Holy Eucharist in two forms. Rite One preserves the Elizabethan English and Rite Two puts virtually the same material into contemporary English. That provision shows the Episcopal acknowledgment of the deep-seated resistance in many church people to liturgical change. In spite of that concession many Episcopalians prefer and continue to use the 1928 Prayer Book.

It is the central commitment to a Prayer Book liturgy that has been the strength of the Episcopal church. The Prayer Book is the means whereby the church connects itself with the past and incorporates what it considers the worthy work of the present. The Prayer Book makes it certain that the church will be spared from the whims or inadequacies of the rector (pastor). There is variety of kind in the worship of Episcopalians. There are "low" churches, in which Protestant influence is most obvious, with morning prayer and the sermon as the regular service, and with little or no actions commonly regarded as Roman Catholic (Sign of the Cross, genuflecting, chanting of Scripture and prayer). There are "high" or Anglo-Catholic churches, in which the Mass would include everything in a Roman Catholic church except the acknowledgment of the pope. Yet in both instances the basic form and content of the service would come from the Prayer Book. The ritual additions would make the difference.

Our study of worship should allow us to make room for a prayer book church. The one major objection by other Christians is the lack of spontaneity that a prayer book creates. However, that is a matter of taste and preference, not theology. To be sure, there is place given by the Prayer Book to spontaneous prayer, though it is not widely used. Yet nothing in Scripture prohibits prescribed prayer and ritual. Like anything in the church, and especially in worship, what is oft-repeated is capable of abuse and the deadness of routine. There are certainly built-in hazards to prayer book worship. Yet we discover that hazards are universal, and many non-Episcopal ministers have discovered the beauty and effectiveness of prayers and ritual that are carefully and creatively planned and written.

1. Explore your hymnal for Luther's hymns, German chorales, and works by Bach.
2. Have you or any of the group been in Lutheran worship? Share the experience. Why would it be said that Luther was not a radical reformer when it came to worship?
3. Buy or borrow an Episcopal Book of Common Prayer. The marriage and burial services will have many familiar lines. You might also secure a bulletin from an Episcopal church and see how the Prayer Book is used.
4. Again, a visit to an Episcopal church, or a visit by a priest or lay leader would prove most interesting.

---

[1]Quoted from the preface to the "Deutsche Messe," *The Works of Martin Luther,* Vol. 6 (Philadelphia: Muhlenberg, 1932) p. 172.

9

Directed Worship: Reformed and Methodist

We have named the second cluster of worship traditions arising from the Reformation "directed worship" because the worship forms of those Christians is more suggested by their leadership than required or prescribed. It is true that even the Lutheran and Episcopal churches have a great deal to say about their form of worship, but the second group exercises even more congregational choices. There are guidelines, but they are not always considered.

1. Reformed (Presbyterian) Worship

There is a very specific approach to worship that traces its roots to the great Swiss reformer, John Calvin. Calvin's theology has formed the beliefs and practices of millions of Christians in the Reformed tradition. They would include Presbyterian churches of many different groups, Reformed, and Christian Reformed churches.

It would be interesting but not completely relevant for us to consider the ideas of some reformers who influenced Calvin. They would include Zwingli, whose interpretation of the Lord's Supper and baptism was and is very influential, and others such as William Farel and Martin Bucer. Suffice it to say that this French scholar, John Calvin (1509–1564), came to Geneva in 1541 after spending three years in Strasbourg. In Strasbourg he did his first serious work as a worship leader, and the service book that Bucer had written in Strasbourg was very important to Calvin.

At least two things were significant for the future of the Reformed church. One was the formation of a service that could omit the Eucharist even though its structure was intended to include it. By strange turns of history, that idea became especially influential in the Scottish church, as we shall see. The other was the practice of psalmody, the use of metrical psalms for the singing of the congregation, rather than the use of hymns.

In Geneva Calvin wrote a treatise called "The Form of Church Prayers and Hymns with the Manner of Administering the Sacraments and Consecrating Marriage According to the Custom of the Ancient Church." The liturgy, which he said was "generally used," took this form:

Opening Sentence
Confession (Geneva refused Absolution)
Psalm
Collect for Illumination, Lessons, and Sermon
Prayer and Creed

(The Lord's Supper is optional)
Words of Institution
Fencing the Table (Excommunication of offenders and call
    for self-examination)
Sursum Corda ("Lift up your hearts," but modified by Farel)
Communion

Psalm
Thanksgiving
Canticle
Benediction
(Alms were received following the service)

We need a word or two of explanation about this service. Calvin did not originally intend the Sunday service to exclude communion. The church leaders, however, refused a weekly Eucharist, and Calvin agreed to a monthly observance. "Fencing the Table" was a lengthy statement that warned all unbelievers, heretics, and gross sinners that they were barred from eating holy food. It also included an exhortation to genuine repentance by all Christians. That sounds a bit somber, but Calvin further suggested a joyful recognition that the grace of Christ is freely offered and that we are never truly worthy.

The *Sursum Corda* ("Lift up your hearts") was the work of Farel and instructed worshipers to

> lift our spirits and hearts on high.... Let us not be fascinated by these earthly and corruptible elements which we see with our eyes and touch with our hands, seeking Him there as though He were enclosed in the bread or wine.... Let us be content to have the bread and wine as signs and witnesses, seeking the truth spiritually where the Word of God promises that we shall find it.

That was Calvin's way of protecting the spiritual nature of the presence of Christ. Probably to remove further any idea of sacrifice or human offering in the Eucharist, alms were received after the service was concluded.

Several elements are important to our understanding of Calvin's theology of worship and how it continued and found its way into churches of today.

Authority. The key, or at least one of the keys, is Calvin's attitude toward authority. Authority for everything the church might do was, for Calvin, derived from Scripture and the ancient church. That view gave warrant for rejection of the practices of Rome that Calvin considered a perversion of the gospel. It also demanded that the church preserve to the limit of its ability the practice and form of the apostolic community. That principle underlies Calvin's rejection of hymnody in favor of the use of psalms in worship. He was on certain ground with psalms, but looked upon any contemporary expression as inferior.

Revelation. Calvin's principle of authority led logically to his great focus on the revealed Word of God. Worship, like everything else in the church, was nothing if it did not unfold the treasures of the Word. The Word of God was the greatest gift of God to the church. The Word of God was nothing less than God revealed to us in Christ. Therefore, nothing could be more important or more glorious than to hear and receive the Word of God. That meant that for Calvin Word and sacrament were really one. Preaching was a kind of sacrament of the Word of God and the Eucharist was a sacrament of the Word of God. Eucharist derived its meaning and significance from the Word, and without that Word being received and obeyed the Eucharist was nothing at all. Although Calvin had no desire to separate Word and sacrament, his theology was not offended by the subordination of the sacrament to the Word. That meant that the reading and preaching of the Word were the indispensable realities for meaningful worship.

Understanding. If all this is true, then the primary means of attaining the objective of all worship, the adoration of God, is to *understand* the Word that is given to us. For Calvin this placed the center of worship in the mind or spirit. Accordingly, the externals were at best unnecessary, or at worst a hindrance to the spiritual exercise of worship. Calvin valued order, but only so that we would be free to concentrate on the internal, spiritual realities of God and His Word. That is not to say that Calvin did not value the sacraments. He would do so for nothing other than their biblical basis. But their value was in their potential for deeper understanding of the grace of God mediated to us in Christ. It is in believing the promises of Christ that He will indeed make us partakers of His body and blood, which is accomplished spiritually in our souls. It would seem inevitable that a worship that centers on the Word would tend to be cerebral, a matter of understanding and knowing.

Worship. Worship for Calvin was the proper expression of the body of Christ. His concern for the body in the presence of its Lord was that it should be pure and holy. This brought a penitential quality to worship, especially in the presence of a sovereign God. Yet no one excelled Calvin in the joyous proclamation of the grace of God. Neither was he excelled in his stern warning to offenders and solemn confessions and recitations of the law. Great was his desire to maintain a pure church.

Those who followed Calvin have fairly well preserved his approaches to worship, although some of the direct descendants are less loyal at times than the marginal relatives. It is fair to say that worship for Calvin was serious and earnest.

That same attitude, especially toward ceremonial matters, went to the English-speaking world via John Knox and Scotland. The Scottish church used the Book of Common Prayer of 1549 and 1552 for good reason. John Knox had influenced its formation. So had Peter Martyr and Martin Bucer, who taught at Oxford and Cambridge at the invitation of Cranmer. But in 1553, when Mary Tudor, a Roman Catholic, became queen, Knox fled to Frankfurt and then to Geneva. With Calvin's help he drew up a liturgy that was used by the English refugees in Geneva and returned with it to Scotland in 1559. It became the Book of Common Order in 1564 and was official in the Scottish church until 1645.

The book was an honest preservation of the Geneva liturgy. But there were two changes. One was the provision for a *lectio continua,* an orderly reading of books of the Bible and preaching from them. Knox rejected the Christian Year as a form for worship. The other change was further reduction of the Eucharist to four times a year. That meant that the pulpit far outweighed the table in prominence, though both were present in the church.

The Scottish church also followed Geneva in using tables for the Lord's Supper. That idea agreed with Knox, who abhorred the practice of kneeling to receive the sacrament. The Nonconformists in England remained in their pews for communion, a practice continued in most of the Reformed churches today.

That brings us to the major worship forming event in the Reformed church in England, Scotland, and America—the Westminster Assembly and its *Directory for the Public Worship of God*, published in 1644. But to understand that event, we must mention the Puritans, whose influence in America is well known.

Puritanism was a continuation and extension of Calvinism in England. It was not a separate organization, but was a particular party, both in the church and in the state. On the question of authority the Puritans, with Calvin, looked more to Scripture only, and the Anglican church, with Luther, looked more to Scripture and tradition. The focus of the issue as it pertained to worship was, of course, the Book of Common Prayer. The Puritans were not against using a book; they just wanted to reform the book on what they considered were biblical grounds. That meant the elimination of "Romish" practices—such things as vestments, the sign of the Cross in baptism, kneeling to receive the sacrament, and the use of the ring in marriage. It wasn't just the presence of those matters, however, as it was the imposition of their use through the mandate of the Book of Common Prayer. The Puritans wanted a directory, a guidebook, rather than specified liturgy. And that is exactly what they got through the Parliament in 1645, the Westminster Directory.

The Puritans felt that the Directory served to finish the Anglican reformation that had begun a hundred years earlier. It was very similar to the Scottish Book of Common

Order and it made a strong point of preserving "free prayer." It claimed to provide ministers with "some help and furniture"; yet it allowed them to bring to their congregations the relevance, timeliness, and godly model of extempore prayer.

Special attention was given to directions for preaching. Some had taken to running commentaries on the Scripture lessons, and that was forbidden. The preacher was expected to know Greek and Hebrew and to be skilled in biblical understanding, theology, and the arts and sciences. The Lord's Prayer was recommended as a "pattern of prayer," which allowed its omission, and as a "comprehensive prayer," which allowed its inclusion. The Gloria, Creed, and Ten Commandments were not included in the liturgy.

There is really nothing of significance in the history of Reformed worship for the next two hundred years. In Scotland, and through Scotland to America, the Presbyterian churches were generally considered nonliturgical. Indeed, the services of the Church of Scotland finally became a stolid and eventually stodgy and dreary repetition of poorly composed prayers and interminable sermons. In the middle of the nineteenth century there were stirrings and rustlings for worship renewal, which also reached to America. In 1876 Henry Van Dyke, Sr., asked for the preparation of new service forms, but it was 1906 before anything emerged. The book was "voluntary" and therefore resistible. Opposition was largely from the pew. Revisions came in 1928 and 1944.

The most recent worship guide for Presbyterians was issued in 1970, *The Worshipbook: Services and Hymns*. It was a joint effort by the Cumberland Presbyterian Church, The Presbyterian Church in the United States (Southern Presbyterian), and the United Presbyterian Church in the United States of America. The book contains recommended outlines for use when sacraments are included and a Lord's Day service without sacrament. Marriage, funeral, ordination, and commissioning services are also given. There are litanies on various topics, readings, and collects for the Christian Year, and a lectionary. The major part of the book is a collection of hymns and responses, which the editors identify as specifically chosen for use in the services outlined, especially the Lord's Day service, rather than a general collection.

The following is the outline for a Lord's Day service without the sacrament:

BASIC STRUCTURE	ADDITIONS AND VARIANTS
Call to Worship	
	Versicle (a verse or portion of Scripture)
Hymn of Praise	
Confession of Sin	
Declaration of Pardon	
Response	(Gloria, Hymn, or Psalm)
Prayer for Illumination	(Or, the Collect for the Day)
Old Testament Lesson	
	Anthem, Canticle, or Psalm
New Testament Lesson(s)	
Sermon	
	Ascription of Praise
	An Invitation
Creed	
	Hymn
	Concerns of the Church
The Prayers of the People	
The Peace	
Offering	
	Anthem or Special Music
	Doxology or Response
Prayer of Thanksgiving	
The Lord's Prayer	
Hymn	
Charge	
Benediction	

It would be fair to observe that by no means do all Presbyterian churches follow that order, nor is it required that they do so. It continues to be a Directory. It recommends weekly Eucharist, but that is not followed now any more than for Calvin. The sermon is the central event in most Presbyterian churches, and the pastoral prayer is more a continuing tradition from Knox than the prayers of the people. Many churches are using the lectionary, and the chances are very good that you would hear at least one reading from it on any given Sunday in most Presbyterian churches.

There is ongoing work on *The Worshipbook*, especially in the matter of alleged sexist language. It was published just before such issues were being raised.

Worship in the Presbyterian church is the responsibility of the pastor (teaching elder) and the session (elders).

2. Methodist (Wesleyan) Worship

John Wesley, much like Martin Luther, did not set out to be a reformer of the worship forms of his church. Wesley was an Anglican clergyman, and in the earlier days of his leadership he directed his "Methodists" to attend the regular Anglican church services. The services were "supplemented" by Methodist preaching services, which were held at 5:00 A.M. and 5:00 P.M. on Sunday—a testimony to the high level of Methodist zeal.

It isn't difficult to understand why the regular Anglican churches were not all that happy with the Methodists. The growing chilliness produced the Methodist "Chapel." Once they had what was essentially their own church, the 5:00 A.M. service was deleted, but the evening gathering remained popular. At that meeting the Methodists enjoyed a very simple, almost Puritan type of service: hymns, Scripture lessons, prayers given spontaneously, and sermons.

To be sure, Wesley attempted to retain a strong Church of England pattern for the regular Sunday worship, but the new wine of the evangelical awakening for him demanded new forms. Wesley introduced such events as the "love feast," a communal meal, and the "Covenant Service," a very moving and positive act of Christian commitment. There were also the "class meetings," a kind of early small-group gathering that demanded a high level of Christian discipline and mutual accountability. Sunday school and fellowship meetings were also a vital part of church life.

Above all, Methodist worship was energized by hymns, and all agree that hymns were the "liturgy" of Methodism. John and Charles Wesley published *Hymns and Sacred Poems* in 1739 and began a tradition that has affected the entire church ever since. We will discuss hymns and music in worship later, but we should notice that Wesley was anxious for all aspects of Christian life and teaching to be expressed in song.

Luther had especially emphasized hymns as alternatives for specific parts of the Mass. Wesley expanded that idea and had a hymn for almost any conceivable doctrine or life situation. His love for the Eucharist was demonstrated by the fact that his hymnal eventually provided 145 hymns for that service. It should be noted that the bulk of the work was done by John's brother Charles who penned more than six thousand hymns in his lifetime.

In 1784 Wesley sent to America "The Sunday Services of the Methodist Church in North America with Other Occasional Services." It was really almost a duplication of the Book of Common Prayer of 1662. The American Methodists did not share Wesley's enthusiasm, however, and in 1792 published their own "Discipline," which completely dropped such Anglican practices as morning and evening prayer, psalms, collects, and the Epistle and Gospel for the Lord's Supper.

It is not difficult to understand that kind of development. Methodism was a frontier religion with "circuit-riding" preachers, so well exemplified in Bishop Francis Asbury. Evangelistic pioneering pushed the Methodists from the smallest to the largest church body in America in the span of fifty years (1794-1844). 1844 marked the division of the church into North and South, but reunion took place in 1939.

By 1920 the Methodist church had become largely middle class and more formal in its worship. The "Gothic revival" was on in church architecture, and the church was caught up in first an aesthetic and then a historical emphasis in its worship forms. There was no particular commitment to a worship directory, but in 1944 the first in a series of worship books was published. It was revised in 1964 and again in 1972. That year marked the appearance of the series, Supplemental Worship Resources. By 1980 ten had been published and eleven more were projected through 1983. Number ten is called "We Gather Together"; it includes a Sunday Service (Word and Table) and service orders for baptism, confirmation and renewal, Christian marriage, and a funeral (called a service of death and resurrection).

The keys to the approach to Methodist worship are pluralism and flexibility. There is a serious attempt to return to the basic form of Word and Table that echoes the Book of Common Prayer. But there is genuine recognition of varying church circumstances and ample provision for variety. The service order recommended follows a basic pattern:

Entrance and Praise
Proclamation and Praise
Response and Offerings
The Holy Meal (Optional)
Sending Forth

From that pattern is suggested the following order:

Gathering
Greeting
Hymn of Praise
Opening Prayer(s)
Act of Praise
Prayer for Illumination
Scripture Lection
Psalm or Anthem
Scripture Lection
Hymn or Song
Gospel Lection
Sermon
Response to the Word
Concerns and Prayers
The Peace
Offering
Prayer of Thanksgiving
    or Communion
Lord's Prayer
Hymn or Song
Dismissal with Blessing
Going Forth

Various alternatives or possible omissions are given throughout. The "Response to the Word" can include an invitation to discipleship, a hymn, baptism, creed, or confession and pardon.

As in all our churches, the form of worship may vary considerably from one to another, but we have seen how an affinity for the form outlined in the worship directory might be present in Methodist churches. The tradition of a vital hymnody is certainly treasured by Methodists, though not easy to preserve.

STUDY GUIDE

1. What was the basis for Reformed worship becoming "sermon-centered"?
2. Find some "metrical psalms" in the hymnbook. There are always settings of Psalm 23. Why did Presbyterians sing the Psalms?
3. All of our churches are indebted to the Wesleys. Find their work in your hymnal.
4. Methodist churches have been widely diverse, depending on the particular setting. Use any experience of the group to explore Methodist worship.

10

Open Worship: Baptist, Congregational, Churches of Christ, and Independent

We move now to a very large and quite recent segment of Protestant churches, one with great organizational diversity, but with a basic unity in its approach to worship. It could take various names—"free," indicating that it has no fixed ecclesiastical control; "congregational," in that each local church is considered autonomous; "spontaneous" or "extemporaneous," in that some premium is laid upon the immediate activity of the Spirit in worship; or "nonliturgical," in that the worship tends to consider itself unstructured as to content.

I have chosen to call this "open" worship, although the preceding terms are probably equally good. That term does emphasize the lack of regulation and helps us remember that the worship is given constant opportunity to arise from the theological and cultural preferences of each particular group.

1. Baptist Worship

It is common to assume that the Baptists must have some relationship to the Anabaptists, a large group of rather radical believers of the sixteenth century Reformation. *Ana* means "again," and these were the people who rejected infant baptism and required their followers to be baptized as believing adults. That movement was known for such radical ideas as the belief in the sharing of possessions and the stand against participation in war. One Anabaptist group followed the teachings of Menno Simons of Holland in the sixteenth century. From that beginning have come the Mennonites, many of whom are in the United States where they have continued a tradition of social service and opposition to war. Another group that emerged from the Anabaptist movement is the Amish community of Pennsylvania.

The Baptist churches, however, more properly trace their tradition through the English Separatists. A forefather of that movement was Reverend John Smyth, who was influenced by the Mennonites and pastored a body of believers in Amsterdam in 1608. In 1611 some of his congregation moved to England and became the General Baptists. It was not long before some of the Baptists also moved to America.

John Smyth's writing about the worship of the English Baptists is very interesting:

1. We hold that the worship of the New Testament properly so called is spiritual proceeding originally from the heart: and that reading out of a book (though it is a lawful ecclesiastical action) is no part of spiritual worship, but rather the invention of the man of sin, it being substituted for a part of spiritual worship.
2. We hold that seeing prophesying is a part of spiritual worship: therefore in time of prophesying it is unlawful to have the book [i.e., the Bible] as a help before the eye.
3. We hold that seeing singing a psalm is a part of spiritual worship: therefore it is unlawful to have the book before the eye in time of singing a psalm. (W. T. Whitley, *The Works of John Smyth*, 1915, p. 273.)

Evidently that practice was carried out in worship, and after the reading of the text for preaching, the Bible was removed and several sermons were preached with neither Bible nor notes. Prayers were, of course, extemporaneous and psalms were sung from memory. Baptists have not followed Smyth, but the principle is interesting and Smyth was consistent. Services were from 8:00 A.M. to noon and then again from 2:00 to 6:00 in the afternoon!

It is interesting to observe that the early Baptists did not make immersion an issue. Even now some Mennonites baptize by pouring. Adult baptism was the issue, to be sure, but the mode was not prescribed.

The American patriarch of the Baptist churches is Roger Williams. His passion for freedom had both ecclesiastical and political results, and church and state owe him a great debt. The Baptist churches moved West with the expansion of America, and one of the factors of their amazing growth was the effective use of laypersons. The price paid in that process was the repetition of division. That is reflected today in the number of significant Baptist groups. There are the American Baptist Convention (formerly Northern Baptist Convention), Southern Baptist Convention, the Conservative Baptist Association, the Baptist General Conference, and a host of smaller organizations. One adds to this the large number of black Baptist churches, some of which are part of larger conventions, but many of which are completely independent.

The spirit of independence is neither surprising nor all that problematic for Baptists. It must be remembered that for them, and for all who are congregationalist, the full, complete, and truly adequate expression of the church visible in the world is the local church, a specific worshiping congregation. The worship of that church is rooted in its theology. That church must worship in a way that is truly indigenous, and it must assume responsibility for the quality and content of its worship.

The Baptist church in the nineteenth century was even more "revivalistic" than the Methodists. Indeed, from earliest days the Baptists have spawned such great preachers as Bunyan, Spurgeon, and Billy Graham. Baptist worship has a natural inclination to be sermon-centered. Baptism occupies a prominent place in worship, but communion may or may not. It might be celebrated monthly in some places, quarterly in others. It is regarded as a memorial, very much in the theological tradition of Zwingli, the Swiss reformer.

In some Baptist churches the Calvinist practice of "fencing the table" has been made even more stringent. This is known as "closed communion," and the elements are administered only to those who are members in good standing of that particular local church. Some churches that did not monitor the Lord's Table quite that strictly would still follow the practice of "dismissing" people from the gathering after the sermon and before the communion. That practice is reminiscent of the "Mass of the Catechumens" of the early church, which allowed those preparing for baptism (catechumens) to hear the preaching but not to participate in the Eucharist (Mass of the Faithful). The practice is not widespread in Baptist churches today.

Worship in Baptist churches would rarely, if ever, include the recitation of a creed. With the authority for all church matters in the deposit of the local church, the use of nonbiblical formulas from any outside body would be inappropriate.

2. Congregational Worship

We have already noted that there is a basic commonality in the approach to church government and worship between Baptists and Congregationalists. Both groups can trace origins to English Separatists. Congregationalism, however, was more influenced by Calvin and Puritanism. It was also influenced by the Quakers in its desire for Spirit-led worship, especially in the matter of prayers. The objection was to prescribed forms of prayer, and that concern was raised so convincingly that the Congregationalists were probably responsible for the Westminster Assembly adopting a Directory rather than a specific, biblically-based liturgy.

We should also mention the contribution to worship of Isaac Watts, the great hymn writer. In 1673, in Southwark, a Baptist pastor named Benjamin Keach led his congregation, after the Lord's Supper, in the singing of a hymn that he had composed. Others followed with similar composition, but it was Isaac Watts, a Congregational minister, who in 1705 first published his book of hymns, psalms, and poems. It was followed by other volumes in 1707 and 1719. Some were hymns based on Scripture, some were on "divine subjects," and some were metrical versions of the Psalms. He "imitated in the language of the New Testament" the Psalms of David. "Jesus Shall Reign," for instance, is based on Psalm 72, but Watts made it a Christian song. "Joy to the World" is based on Psalm 98. We are all obviously still singing the hymns of Isaac Watts.

Congregationalism moved to America with the Pilgrims, and by the beginning of the nineteenth century, they were the largest and most influential religious group. Then came the division of their forces by the Unitarians. Since that time the Congregationalists have been seriously affected by the onslaughts of rationalism. The classical forms of worship were being replaced by well-prepared prayers and set liturgies. Both England (1920) and America (1948) produced service books. In America, church mergers produced the present United Church of Christ.

The vitality of the earlier Congregational church is now probably seen in the many independent churches in America. Congregationalism as a worship tradition is in reality now closer to the "directed" style than the "open." It would not disdain the use of a creed, for instance, but it would feel free to change it, or frequently to replace it.

3. The Churches of Christ

Another group of churches with an "open" tradition, usually of Congregational structure, traces its roots to Alexander Campbell. The Disciples of Christ, the Church of Christ, and the Christian Church are all part of this very interesting collection, and their influence upon American worship tradition is significant.

Campbell, a Scottish Presbyterian, came to some very strong theological conclusions in 1809. He began his search for a church that was truly a New Testament body. That meant several things to him: each local group should be autonomous; distinctions between lay and clergy were wrong and should be eliminated; creeds were unscriptural; baptism by immersion of believers was proper; and the Lord's Supper should be a part of Sunday worship.

Those ideas, though modern, were not really new in the ecclesiastical landscape, and when Campbell arrived in America there were Baptists who vigorously agreed with him. However, he felt the Baptists had gone too far in building ecclesiastical machinery. So Campbell established a new group that was, in a sense, committed to not being a group. Even the name was a problem. "Christians" seemed clear and biblical enough, but Campbell favored "Disciples." Both terms have persisted. Another group, "Church of Christ" (also a New Testament phrase), pulled out over the issue of musical instruments in the meeting houses. There were other controversies as well, but all persisted in worship that was unique in church history. Campbell rejected the emotionalism that accompanied the revivals of the Western frontier, but he saw the biblical significance of keeping preaching and the Lord's Supper together and of keeping worship open to active participation by all.

Until 1920 the worship in the "restorationist" churches would follow, by and large, the pattern listed here:

Opening praise
Scripture lessons
Pastoral prayer (Extempore)
Communion, which would include a brief homily, prayer by
   an elder over the bread, and prayer by another elder over
   the cup
Offering
Sermon

After World War II the order was changed in that the communion and sermon were transposed. In 1953 a Service Book was published for Christian churches, a rather far cry from the original ideas of Campbell. But the church had gone through the process of institutionalization and was in reality one of the establishment denominations of the Protestant churches. It shared in the Gothic revival of the 1920s and has been a participant in the Consultation on Church Union.

There is really no other Protestant group that has consistently kept the Eucharist and preaching together in the worship of the church as a regular event. Some in that church complain that the observance of the Lord's Supper is too routine and casual. Yet that can be said about most items of liturgy at some time or other. The church has also maintained an important place for baptism.

4. Other Denominations and Independent Churches

There are numbers of groups and individual churches we could consider in this survey. Nearly all will reflect some ties to one of the traditions we have already considered, though each will probably have moved away from that tradition, especially theologically. Usually the pattern of worship is more readily retained. (We exclude from these the "charismatic" or Pentecostal churches, which we consider in our next chapter.)

Examples are in order. From the Lutheran churches in Scandinavia came the "nonstate" or Free church that, in coming to America, became the Swedish Covenant, now Evangelical Covenant church. Its worship was influenced by pietism, revival, and reaction against liturgical formalism. The Evangelical Free church had very similar roots.

There are numbers of groups emerging from the Methodist tradition. The Church of the Nazarene, the Wesleyan church, and the Free Methodists are all theological revisions of Methodism. In most instances that meant a move toward less structure, both ecclesiastically and liturgically. The push for purity of doctrine usually results in a renewed emphasis on the pulpit and sermon-centered worship. That renewal reflects a genuine concern for the teaching ministry of the church.

Other denominational groups have particular worship practices that attempt to duplicate New Testament or early church tradition. The (Grace) Brethren church, for instance, practices trine immersion. The idea of three "washings," in the name of Father, Son, and Holy Spirit, is very ancient. The Brethren church also practices "foot washing," usually annually.

There are thousands of Christians who meet for worship and service in "independent" churches. These are of necessity congregationally governed. They are usually close to Baptist or Congregational tradition. Since they are formed as "nondenominational" or "interdenominational" churches, they gather people with varied worship traditions and often attempt to recognize those traditions in their worship life. Often they will permit and practice all types of baptism. Worship services will tend to informality, although even that may change, depending on the pastor or people. Such churches are usually the result of strong leaders, and the worship is usually sermon-centered. The style suggests a relatively recent formation and a limited theological and historical understanding of worship, since worship is almost never the basis for the formation of each particular church.

Such wide possibilities for individual church variety make generalizations most inadequate. Some independent churches are firmly set in a solid and well-perceived worship tradition, and some have little concept of the meaning of the gathered church beyond the opportunity to hear another extended Bible lesson. We will discover that this is not all bad, but I hope we will also discover the rich possibilities for improvement in any worshiping community.

STUDY GUIDE

1. Open worship puts a great premium on spontaneity. What contributions can this make, and what problems can it offer?

2. What view of baptism is reflected in most Baptist churches? What are the historical roots for Baptists?

3. Who is responsible for Baptist worship? What is "closed communion"?

4. How has the United Church of Christ somewhat changed Congregational tradition?

5. What is the distinguishing mark of Disciples or Christian church worship?

6. Compare the experiences of the group with the churches mentioned in section four. The Independent church is especially American. Why?

11

Charismatic Worship: Pentecostals, Neo-Pentecostals, and Quakers

There is a temptation to discuss worship traditions under three "centers": altar-centered—Roman, Orthodox, Lutheran, and Episcopalian; pulpit-centered—Reformed, Methodist, Baptist, Congregational, and their relatives; and congregation-centered—the charismatics. But those categories are too neat, and they break down under closer scrutiny. If we talk about a table rather than an altar, most churches have them. All traditions will include a pulpit and it is to be hoped that all traditions value the participation of the people. However, in point of emphasis, and in point of the distinctive in the understanding of worship, the terms might stand.

We are looking now at a tradition of worship that is primarily an expression of the Spirit, both in leader and people. That is an area largely staked out by what are termed "Pentecostals," but historical developments dictate that we include "Neo-Pentecostals." That makes our classification a twentieth century phenomenon, and I will explain later why I am also including the three-hundred-year-old Quakers in the group.

1. Pentecostals

Most Pentecostal churches acknowledge their debt to the Azusa Street Prayer Meeting in Los Angeles in 1906. That meeting was part of a particular religious revival that also occurred in Kansas and finally was carried to the entire

United States and many places abroad. It was termed "Pentecostal" because it was the experience of the overwhelming reality of the Holy Spirit that was accompanied by ecstatic outbursts of praise to God, including prayer, weeping, laughing, singing, and the language of ecstasy known as "tongues."

Once again Christians developed their theological definition and understanding out of the experience of worship. It is important that we remember the great significance of experience in worship for the interpretation of Scripture and the formulation of theology. It was not a difficult task at all for the Pentecostals to move from the exciting and significant experience of their worship to biblical affirmations that those were indeed visitations of the Spirit. That is not to depreciate their interpretation, but rather to observe that we all discover that *lex orandi est lex credendi*—"it is out of our praying that our faith is defined."

Numerous church groups, including a large number of black churches, emerged from that beginning. The most significant denomination, and probably most representative, is the Assemblies of God. That group was organized in 1914 and in a short ten years was also functioning in Great Britain and Ireland. The genius of the church was in its recognition, indeed its expectation, of the exercise of the gifts of the Spirit in the entire congregation. The expectation arose from the teaching that all Christians subsequent to their conversion could and should experience the "baptism of the Spirit according to Acts 2:4."

It was further expected that that baptism would be evidenced by speaking in tongues, the expression of an ecstatic language, the utterance of the Spirit. Receiving the gift was defined as a specific event, like conversion, and the speaking in tongues might never again occur, nor would it be needed. There would follow, however, gifts of the Spirit, one of which might be tongues, but it might also be one of the many other gifts of the Spirit to the church—interpretation, prophecy, healing, faith, or giving.

The openness of the Assemblies to the gifts is well demonstrated in their worship. Prayer as the expression of the whole church is uttered aloud by all. That "concert" prayer is not unknown in other cultures, and once experienced does not become as disconcerting as it might sound. It is very easy to see how a public prayer led by one person, accompanied by expressions of "Amens" and other notes of involvement, would soon become almost indistinguishable. The worshiper will usually end up framing and expressing his own prayer under the direction of the Spirit.

Prayer for the sick, including anointing and the "laying on of hands," is also a possible part of worship, as well as some messages to the church through "tongues," which would see one individual "speaking" and another "interpreting." That practice in the Assemblies has grown increasingly more controlled, but it is generally not repressed. There might also be a "prophecy," some message of import to the church or individuals.

Earlier, preaching was often the privilege of any, but the Assemblies have developed a clergy that carries the preaching responsibility, and it is increasingly well-trained and qualified.

One practice that the Assemblies have borrowed from frontier Protestantism is the time of prayer at the front of the church in the concluding part of a service. It might be at a railing or in the pews or seats. The gathering is for any kind of spiritual concern, and participants might include those seeking an experience of conversion or baptism of the Spirit, or those wishing prayer for themselves, friends, or family, or those requesting healing. For many, those frequent visits to a place of special prayer are very helpful.

The leaders of the Assemblies of God and other Pentecostal groups will emphasize the reality of spontaneity in their worship. There will often be opportunity given for individuals to share experiences of grace or expressions of praise and thanks to God. There might come times of prayer, testimony, confession, and singing, which become increasingly emotional and rise in very discernible levels to a crescendo of release and joy.

That is not to say that all those ingredients will be in every service of all Pentecostal churches. There may well be a very orderly Protestant-type preaching service, with hymns, prayers, offerings, Scripture, and sermon. Many Pentecostal churches have a more predictable pattern to their weekly worship than they would care to admit. Yet, eventually, the openness of the meeting to the spontaneous movings of the Spirit would be manifested. Otherwise, the church would feel itself cold and unfruitful.

Latin America and Africa have witnessed an amazing expansion of Pentecostal congregations in the last half of the twentieth century. One would admit that the cultural expressiveness in both continents would find Pentecostal worship fulfilling. Even the more staid and formal groups of Europe and America find their sister congregations in Africa or Latin America, or even India and Asia, far more informal and spontaneous. On a recent visit the pope was startled to discover what African music and dancing have done to the Mass. Such worship is often without a particular theology of the Spirit that would call for such a model. It is indigenous to the people, however, and strongly influenced by their culture.

2. Neo-Pentecostals

For some time church leaders tended to explain the phenomenon of the Pentecostals as a psychological, or even sociological, piece of data. There were attempts to show that the adherents were usually economically and socially deprived, with little opportunity for personal expression through artistic or cultural means. It was assumed that the repression of feeling in drab circumstances called for emotional release, and that this accounted for the ecstatic language, shouting, weeping, dancing, and general boisterousness of Pentecostal worship.

A movement in the churches beginning in the 1950s brought an end to such surmising. That movement is now called Neo-Pentecostalism. It may also be called charismatic, a term that was not generally applied to the Pentecostal movement, though it might well have been. Charismatic comes from the Greek word *charismata*, meaning "gifts." It merely emphasizes the expectation of the Pentecostals that all the gifts of the Spirit are for the present ministry of the church. All churches believe in some *charismata*. Pentecostals believe in all of the gifts and think that all the gifts are for today.

Neo-Pentecostals, however, have also—like earlier Pentecostals—experienced some further work of the Spirit in them beyond baptism and confirmation. In most instances this "baptism of the Spirit" was evidenced by *glossolalia*, the gift of tongues. But unlike earlier Pentecostals, many kept on using that ability, either as a vehicle of address to the church through interpretation, or as the language of private prayer and praise. Another interesting change that brings on the title "neo" is that very often the charismatics did not see it their calling to leave their particular group, for example, Episcopal, Presbyterian, Lutheran, Methodist, Baptist, or Roman Catholic.

The Roman Catholic and Protestant denominations have had varied reactions to the charismatic development. The Roman church has probably led the way in acceptance, understanding, and concern, without fully embracing the movement. There are many priests and not a few bishops who profess to be charismatic. The effect on the

Mass has been minimal, although charismatic parishes will have some gatherings, usually Bible studies and possibly a Eucharist, that will include spontaneous praise and manifestations of spiritual gifts, such as tongues and prophecy. The same could be found in the Episcopal church, but in most situations the unique aspects of charismatic worship are in extra meetings that are rather clearly understood to be for that purpose. Otherwise the Neo-Pentecostals satisfy themselves with private devotion and then find great satisfaction in special congresses or conventions of like-minded and like-experienced persons.

The Pentecostals often find it strange that those "baptized with the Spirit" do not more readily gravitate to their churches, which have for decades taught and practiced those doctrines. But in most instances the Catholics, Episcopalians, and Presbyterians profess to find even greater satisfaction in their traditional worship forms, especially if some small concessions are made to their interests.

Both classic and Neo-Pentecostals respond to the possibility of Spirit-directed spontaneity in worship. That has virtually forced other churches to look carefully at that principle, especially as reflected in New Testament worship. The Neo-Pentecostal has closed the door on the assumption that spontaneity, even to the point of enthusiasm, is a "lower class" characteristic of emotionally deprived people.

3. Quakers

To consider the Quakers under the heading of "charismatic" worship may come as a shock to some. I think a brief reflection will show that it is not only appropriate but instructive in our understanding of the riches of worship tradition.

I said earlier that we are in the area of "participation-centered" worship. The Quakers profoundly believed and practiced that. Yet the result of such commitment for them has stood at the opposite end of the spectrum from the Pentecostals. Perhaps the variety of response between the two groups is helpful in our understanding of the operation of the Holy Spirit. It may prevent our defining too narrowly or rigidly what the manifestations of the work of the Spirit really are.

Most of us know about the Quakers, or more properly, the Society of Friends, only from a distance. There are not very many Quakers in the contemporary scene, and many of the Friends' churches have lost much of the earlier tradition. But the influence of Friends on American life has been profound, both in worship and in social concern.

The history of the church begins with George Fox in the middle of the seventeenth century. He became a "minister" in spite of his lack of ordination and qualification, because he was convinced of the absolute equality of all Christians in all matters relating to the Christian faith. That democratic attitude extended to non-Christians as well. Rather than the customary plural "you," Fox and his followers used "thee" and "thou" in speaking to and about the nobility. "Thou" had been normally reserved for "common" folk, but for the Quakers all were treated alike. The Friends kept that form of speech even when others had dropped it altogether, but the original use was to mark equality, not difference.

Fox recognized no titles and refused to take legal oaths on scriptural grounds. For that nonconformity he was imprisoned eight times. The most illustrious leader of the Friends was William Penn, who received in 1667 a huge tract of land in America from the Crown in settlement of a debt owed to his father. Pennsylvania was that tract, and Penn and his followers became known for the "strange things" that characterized them. They wore broad-brimmed hats, used "thee" and "thou," shunned all warfare and violence, made treaties with the Indians that they kept, and above all, spent long periods in their meeting-houses in silence.

It is the silence that is easily misunderstood and not appreciated. Friends took very seriously the continued presence of Christ by the Spirit in every Christian. The gathered community could do nothing better than offer itself, collectively and individually, for the gracious moving of the Spirit and then await the revelation. Christ's presence was spoken of as the Inner Light, and one radical idea was that women shared the gift and privilege equally with men.

The concentration on inner revelation made silence not only acceptable but necessary. Externals, including words, were completely secondary to the real experience by all of the presence of the Spirit. The implication was that no external rite or action could effect a spiritual change, and the sacraments were not so much removed as spiritualized. Their understanding of the true baptism of the New Covenant was the baptism of the Spirit. The command of Jesus to "do this in remembrance of me" was a spiritual reality for all eating and drinking. There were, therefore, no prescribed external forms, no ordination of any special persons in the church, and no sacraments.

The history of the Friends in America is fascinating, especially in its witness to Christ in the issues of treatment of the Indians, slavery, war, and the equality of women. Friends' churches attracted many during the rise of various peace movements. A great many of the larger evangelical Friends' churches have now called pastors and are virtually indistinguishable from other Congregational or independent churches. But in the meetinghouses of the traditional Friends there are still a quiet waiting upon the Spirit and a fellowship of people who deeply respect the value and function of every person.

Silence is a response to God that is difficult in our contemporary world. We shall look at it further as we attempt to gather the ingredients that make for meaningful worship.

STUDY GUIDE

1. Experience will influence attitudes about charismatic worship. Share your experiences and examine them in light of the chapter.
2. What have been your general impressions about charismatic worship? Have any of these changed as a result of reading this chapter? If so, how?
3. Have you ever been to a Quaker meeting? There are different kinds, of course, but the traditional ones with lots of silence and lots of participation are most interesting.
4. How do you react to silence in a service? Why is it an appropriate part of corporate worship?
5. What do you consider the contribution of the charismatic tradition to the church as a whole?

12

Symbols and Sacraments

The study of worship is, I believe, the finest way to come at ecumenism, the exploration of our common heritage and our unifying realities. Remember that we have identified worship as the expression of a relationship between God and His people. It is a relationship of love, God revealing Himself in Christ and the Spirit ministering grace to us. We must admit that the means of grace in the relationship of worship might be expected to assume a common, recognizable shape in the experience of all Christians.

I think we will discover that, although some Christians emphasize particular aspects of worship as having greater value and meaning in expressing their relationship with God, there are still many elements that Christians practice in common. We all seek to praise God, to pray, to hear His word, to bring our offering, to obey His commands, and to open our lives in significant ways to God and to each other. It is now our task to turn from the various traditions of worship to those aspects that are considered essential in all traditions.

Symbolism

Probably the greatest single area of differing theological opinion in regard to worship is what some term "sacraments" and others call "ordinances." Roman Catholics—and to a less rigid degree, Orthodox Christians—recognize seven sacraments: baptism, Eucharist (Lord's Supper), confirmation, reconciliation (penance), Holy Orders (ordination), marriage, and prayer for the sick (Extreme Unction). The Protestant Reformation gave the name "sacrament" only to those "established by Christ" (dominical), baptism and Eucharist, but retained certain churchly activities surrounding the latter five events. Further theological discussion exposed differences regarding what the sacraments accomplished and what was their purpose in the church.

We have already referred to the famous encounter between Zwingli and Luther at the town of Marburg, where Luther wrote with chalk on the table top, "This is my body" (*Hoc est corpus meum*). We are also aware of the differences between Christians regarding baptism, both as to who should be baptized and how. We need to look closely at that question to understand our own views and also to appreciate the ideas and practices of our fellow Christians.

Basic to our understanding of the sacraments is that they embrace the valuable principle of symbolism. Here we must quickly be aware that there is no consistency as to what one means by the term *symbolism*. Most of us would say that it refers to an idea or reality beyond or more than itself.

When we think about it, we realize that we are surrounded constantly by symbols. A wedding ring, a flag, and a handshake are some of the more obvious ones. A symbol stands for, represents, or suggests, something else. It can be an action, a word, or an object.

A symbol, by some means or other, is related to another reality. It is "thrown together" (the literal meaning of the word) with another idea and suggests that idea to us. This can be a natural relationship—water as a symbol for cleansing would be an example. It can be an accidental relationship, one that arises uniquely and to some extent artificially. Here I would suggest the "V for Victory" sign from World War II. The letter indicated by the spread between first and second fingers is meaningful only for English speakers and because it arose in a wartime. The letter could stand for other things, but our society has assigned it a primary symbolic meaning. The handshake is a symbol given meaning by convention. We just all agree that it is a symbol of politeness and social grace.

Let's consider for a moment the idea that words are really symbols—visual objects that stand for or suggest something else. We human beings are inveterate symbol-makers, and that capacity may be the most significant single expression of our humanness. Even as you read these "symbols" (which are in reality just so many combinations of marks to make letters and words), the idea that was in my mind is experienced in yours. The word itself is not the idea, and in most instances nothing about the word relates at all to the idea, but our common agreement on the symbol makes it work.

Symbols are considered by some philosophers and psychologists to be extremely important. The psychologist Carl Jung has proposed that the entire race of humankind is possessed of symbols that are in the unconscious mind, and that those symbols constantly emerge in our dreams, our folk tales and fairy stories, and in various other events of human experience.

One could also mention the fields of mathematics, physics, music, and other disciplines in which symbolism is extremely important. But our point is to realize not only the contribution, but also the necessity of symbols in our religious life, especially in our worship.

Sign and Symbol

It would be helpful at this juncture to distinguish symbols from signs. Signs can be regarded as essentially practical, something directed to the eye or ear with a view to personal reaction. Signs convey information. The lighted arrow points up, for example, and we know that the elevator will take us that direction. Signs become almost a shorthand of information. When we discuss the arrow as a means of indicating both motion and direction, we are getting into symbolism, but the "sign" itself is for information leading to action.

Now let's come to the question of symbols and worship. We are back to our discussion of sacraments. It is obvious that humans, being symbol-makers, will bring them into their worship. It seems appropriate that just as word-symbols allow us to share meaningful ideas, so objects and actions can be given similar significance. That has certainly been true for worship.

The Old Testament, especially in matters relating to the tabernacle and Temple, is filled with symbolism. We have seen how that symbolism influenced New Testament actions, and how Jesus began His ministry with the ceremonial washing of baptism, commanded His disciples to baptize, and requested His remembrance in a meal of bread and wine. Paul and Barnabas were sent on their missionary journey with the "laying on of hands" by the elders at Antioch (see Acts 13:2–3). James counseled prayer for the sick with the act of anointing with oil (see James 5:14). Paul suggested Christians greet one another with the "kiss of peace" (see Rom. 16:16).

The church has added other symbols to that list of actions, although that is not to say that such additions were not also the practice in New Testament times. Some actions are simple and straightforward; for example, we may stand to sing, speak, or pray as an act of reverence or honor; we might kneel as an act of obedience and humility. There is value in all these various things, including special actions commanded by Jesus, even though we regard them as "symbols" by which we are moved to remembrance, reflection, participation, even imagination.

Perhaps I can illustrate by describing an encounter between two people. They could be said to "meet" if all that happened was that their eyes met and recognition occurred. It would be much more a meeting if they shook hands, or in the style of many cultures, embraced and kissed. If those actions were accompanied by words of greeting and endearment, it would be all the better. Now all the actions would be symbolic of what each was inwardly feeling, but outward participation would intensify the reality of the relationship.

That is what a large number of Christians wish to say about the actions of the church in worship. They regard the actions and objects used by the church in its worship as helpful reminders or illustrations of spiritual reality—as symbols. I don't think it would be fair to say of them that they believe baptism and the Lord's Supper are *only* symbols. That sounds as though a symbol is meaningless or trivial. Such is not the case. They are deeply committed to a properly expressed "relationship" with Christ, but they are convinced that the relationship must be experienced as inward and spiritual.

Those Christians find great joy in expressing their relationship with Christ through the use of actions and objects He ordained (ordinances), but they would insist that the "invisible grace" symbolized by the "visible form" has its own independent spiritual identity. That invisible grace gives reality to the visible form and not vice versa. Because Christ is present spiritually, we can remember Him in the symbol of bread and wine. Bread and wine do not create or bring about His presence. They are symbols. They are made effective by our perception.

Should We Escape from Symbol?

Let me try to put at ease the minds of those who might be resistant to the idea of symbol. There is really no way to avoid symbols, but they need not be a hindrance to our worship. If we gather in a plain room with four blank walls and a pulpit, then we have made a symbolic statement about our concept of God and the way He is to be worshiped. If we decided to have no room at all, to meet outdoors, we would probably find our minds and emotions overwhelmed by the multiple symbolism of trees, rocks, grass, and sky. We might even feel ourselves in danger of worshiping God's handiwork. And we would then find deep satisfaction in returning to the symbols that so pointedly direct us to Christ and the gospel.

We cannot be symbol-free, and we are wise to use the symbols of our heritage as "windows to heaven" through which we see and adore our exalted Lord.

But let me repeat that many in the church today firmly maintain that all symbols are independent of the reality they demonstrate. The symbols have no significance in or of themselves, but speak eloquently of a spiritual reality that is completely beyond them.

There are plenty of statements from the early church, especially from Augustine, to go along with the "symbolic" view. But we must also look at the thinking and interpretations behind the sacramental view. The word *sacrament* is rather unfortunate. It is a Latin word used by Tertullian in the third century and then by Jerome in the Latin Vulgate Bible to translate the Greek word *mysterion*. A *sacramentum* was a sacred oath taken by a soldier, or a solemn vow to keep a promise.

But as with so many words, this one has acquired a much more significant meaning through usage. Even the Greek term has its problems, because our word *mystery* is not the equivalent of the Greek word. A mystery, in the

New Testament sense, is probably best understood as divine self-disclosure, though that is not the only possibility. It also means something hidden that is now revealed.

In Romans 11:25 Paul spoke of the "mystery" he wanted his readers to understand—the unbelief of Israel. In 1 Corinthians 15:51 the mystery is the resurrection of the believers. In Ephesians 5:32 it is the mystery of Christ and the church as reflected in husband and wife. Christ Himself is the mystery of God in Colossians 2:2. Yet oddly enough the term is not applied in the New Testament to the actions that eventually were called sacraments, or mysteries. But that does not destroy the possibility of such usage.

Defining our Faith

Theological language is always growing. Take the word *trinity*, which never occurs in the New Testament, yet has proved very useful. So those who have developed a more complex theology of sacraments will lean hard on the "mysteries" as acts of divine self-disclosure. The importance to them is the emphasis on divine initiative, that nothing is contributed by us, and everything is done by God.

A better word for us moderns is one also used widely in the Eastern church to denote the sacraments—*the gifts*. This would carry with its meaning the fact that the mysteries come from God and yet are received by us.

Just as in so many other matters of theological definition, the thing that made the church clarify its ideas was heresy. When someone is teaching the wrong doctrine you have to define the right one. The problem in the fourth century was regarding baptism and its practice by a group known as the Donatists (after their leader, Donatus). They had divided from the church over the question of whether a baptism performed by an allegedly ungodly bishop was valid. Augustine argued that it was, since the action was really something done by God, not any human being. That opened the door for the development of the sacramental doctrine, *ex opere operato*, which loosely means "worked by the work itself," indicating that a sacrament is God's work, independent of human instrumentality.

It would be helpful to understand the background for the development of this doctrine. Hebrew tradition is friendly to the idea of God as present in and understood through the very mundane realities of life. God is transcendent, to be sure, stooping even to enter heaven and always above and beyond His creation. But He is also immanent, present in cloud and fire, speaking to and through His prophets, communing with His people in fellowship meals, passing over His people who are guarded by a blood-stained doorpost.

The presence of God was not only real, it was associated with objects (consider the ark of the Covenant and the death of Uzzah for touching it; see 2 Sam. 6:6,7). For the Hebrews, and for us, God was present in history, in His "mighty acts" in the course of human events. Perhaps an illustration is in the magnificent story of Moses and the burning bush (see Ex. 3:1–6). Moses turned aside to see a great wonder, a bush that was afire and yet was not consumed. When fire is in a bush it destroys it, yet this bush was still a bush and filled with fire. So it is with our world and our history. For God to be *in* it without consuming it seems impossible. Yet faith knows God to be present, and it is a mystery.

Those who develop a sacramental theology build on that foundation. They argue that the outward sign is itself part of the reality it signifies. That means God does not merely give us object lessons so that we can see what something is like, but He uses very earthly and ordinary things to be the vehicles of His grace and His very being. It's more than just a "show and tell" time.

An often used illustration is a kiss. One could say that a kiss demonstrates the love of two for each other. But in reality the lovers kiss not just because they love, but also in order to love. There is the inner spiritual reality of love, but there is also loving in the act of affection.

Christ Our Sacrament

Sacramental theologians reason that God can do no better than to convey His grace in and through that which is genuinely a part of our human life and experience. They will probably finally appeal to the fact that God's ultimate revelation of Himself is in the Person of Jesus Christ.

On that point the church in its early centuries remained vague and open. For them Christ was present and revealed His grace and loving service in many ways. They did not seek to be technical about it, but neither were they closed. To be baptized was to be cleansed by the forgiving grace of Christ and it was neither by the water nor apart from it. They invited Jesus to the meal of remembrance, and it was His body and His blood that fed them in the consecrated bread and wine. They prayed for the sick and anointed them; they laid hands on those set aside for particular services. From the writings of the first four or more centuries, there are some statements that we regard as essentially symbolic, and some that are forthrightly sacramental. The important thing to note is that this did not seem to become an issue of contention.

Rationalism and Reactionism

The medieval period witnessed a growing effort to *ex-*

plain and *confine* the presence of grace in actions and objects. The age of rationalism or scholasticism took root. In the twelfth century, sacraments in the Western church were finally declared to be exactly seven. The discussion became very philosophical and complex.

A rationalistic understanding of sacrament is best seen in the Roman Catholic explanation of the presence of Christ in the Eucharist. One has to admit a noble motivation on the part of Thomas Aquinas and others to make divine "mysteries" as precise and rational as possible, but the results have not always been all that helpful to our faith. The process is not difficult to trace. Once the number of sacraments was decided, then there was a specific framework for the dispensation of grace, a carefully defined treasury. The church effectively controlled that necessary treasury by giving the clergy the sole custody of the means of grace (except for emergency baptism and for marriage, both of which could be performed by laypersons). Careful theological formulas were worked out so that each sacrament was celebrated properly. This was considered important since God used those events and objects through which to administer His grace.

All of this served to remove the true significance of the observances further from the people, since the complexity of both their explanation and their ceremony could not be understood by the average person. But that did not matter very much, since it was God who was at work through the sacraments, and the cooperation required was largely that no obstacle be raised by the communicant. The church felt it now had a complete and rational system for providing grace through the sacraments to any Christian—from the cradle to the grave.

Then came the Protestant Reformation. Not only did Luther reduce the sacraments to the two that came to be regarded as truly instituted by Christ (baptism and the Eucharist), but he opened the door for altogether new attitudes toward the two that were kept. This is most clearly seen in the radical redefinitions of Zwingli (whom we mentioned before) and in his battle with Luther over the nature of the Eucharist. Even Calvin wanted to be sure that the attention of the Christian was always moved beyond any earthly elements like water or bread and wine, even though God used them as visible signs to administer grace in a spiritual way.

A symbolic understanding of the sacraments was pushed forward by the intellectual changes of the eighteenth-century movement known as the Enlightenment. That was the beginning of the modern period of scientific method and the Industrial Revolution. It is very easy to understand that it allowed no room for the idea that anything material was the vehicle for some supernatural reality. Scholars could now tear every idea apart and reduce it to the basic building blocks of our universe, and God was not found in the process. Yet the Christian could still find deep religious meaning in the spiritual reality that would be prompted by the observance of the sacraments.

Now, however, the effectiveness of the sacrament would be measured in terms of how well the communicant responded or believed. In baptism the confession and faith of the baptized were the points of the action. In the Eucharist the penitence and "remembrance" of the recipient were prompted by hearing the words, seeing the table, and eating and drinking. That understanding went well with a highly individual and personal expression of faith, an approach that now characterizes much of Protestantism.

Back to the Sources

Christians today will come down on both sides of this Protestant divide. I would like to suggest that the Scriptures and the early church can give us instruction. The traditions stemming from Luther, Calvin, Cranmer, and Wesley were and are in varying degrees sacramentalist. Those traditions have modified but not discarded the principle that God acts in the sacraments, *ex opere operato*, independent of human agency.

If we believe that God has indeed chosen to reveal Himself and administer grace to us by means of objects and actions, then we must remember that we are not thereby allowed the luxury of doing nothing. Both in the Eucharist and in baptism, careful reflection makes that obvious. Active faith and repentance are part of baptism, especially if one links confirmation to baptism. A believing and confessing parent is a proper part of the baptism of an infant.

The Eucharist is a holy meal in the view of the sacramentalist, yet it is no meal at all if it is not eaten, and the grateful communicant is the necessary culmination of the feast. Jesus said that remembrance was in taking and eating. That must be regarded seriously. The sacramentalists remain chastened when they remember what was done to the medieval church by the removal of genuine lay participation in the sacraments.

If, on the other hand, we believe that grace from Christ present is a spiritual reality, which may only be enhanced but not communicated by symbols, we need to consider carefully the mystery and power of symbols in our experience. We probably would not be content to side with a kind of mechanical and purely scientific view of the world. We are certainly open to the "supernatural" in the person of Christ, His miracles, and above all His resurrection. We believe He is present and speaking powerfully in the preaching of the Word (which is a symbol, a kind of "audible" sacrament). So we should be equally open to the gracious work of Christ by the means He has ordained. We may have intellectual difficulties in explaining the real presence of Christ, but we certainly don't want to be found defending His real absence.

Just such considerations as these are bringing new vitality and meaning to the place of symbols and sacraments in the worship life of the church. On one hand it is a recovery of mystery and the discovery of an antidote to the secularization of a scientific, technological age. On the other hand, it is the recovery of lay participation in the church, as all the people of God become engaged in the work of worship and in the discovery of the fullness of that worship in Word and sacrament. We enter in by faith.

I find here, as in so many areas of Christian experience, that for all of us the Spirit is probably saying something we need to hear in the thought and action of that "other" group. Our traditions are seldom wrong, although they are often incomplete or impoverished. I think that is best seen in the difficulty of finding a balance between Word and sacrament in the entire church—Protestant, Roman, and Orthodox. When the Word is taken seriously and the significance of preaching is thereby elevated, the value and meaning of sacraments often suffer. When sacraments are looked upon as meaningful encounters with the living Christ, then often preaching seems neglected or disregarded. The fact is, we can have it both ways.

STUDY GUIDE

1. Have you ever thought of words as symbols? That means nearly all thought and communication is "symbolic." What other symbols can you suggest as part of our common life and experience?
2. Most churches include various symbols in their archi-

tecture and decoration. List those you can observe in your church.

3. If "beauty is in the eye of the beholder," what is necessary in the participant to make baptism and communion meaningful or effective?

4. How do you feel about the idea that the significance of baptism or the Eucharist is not dependent on the insight or action of the participant?

5. Discuss the significance of the person celebrating or leading baptism or the Eucharist.

6. How does the sacramentalist use the incarnation of Jesus to validate his view?

13

Your Attitude Toward Worship

Our task now is to put to use in our own experience the many different traditions and the basic biblical truth that we have surveyed concerning worship. That is really the whole point of our study.

It is not enough to look at the fascinating history of the church at worship. Nor is it enough to consider the differing theological ideas that have formed the traditions. The question, indeed the quest, must be to make our worship a way of life and, regardless of our tradition, something that is full, beautiful, and rewarding. I think every Christian wants that. If you have persevered in this reading and study, you obviously do.

I deeply believe that your own personal attitudes and insights can transform a liturgical wilderness into a garden of worship beauty. For most of us, the ingredients of meaningful worship are all there, though they may be poorly expressed, and it is our challenge and our privilege to understand and utilize them.

Annie Dillard shows a bit of what I mean in this excerpt from her book, *Teaching a Stone to Talk*:

Week after week I was moved by the pitiableness of the bare linoleum-floored sacristy which no flowers could cheer or soften, by the terrible singing I so loved, by the fatigued Bible readings, the lagging emptiness and dilution of the liturgy, the horrifying vacuity of the whole, which existed alongside, and probably caused, the wonder of the fact that we came; we returned; we showed up; week after week, we went through with it....Week after week we witness the same miracle: that God is so mighty he can stifle his own laughter....Does anyone have the foggiest idea what sort of power we so blithely invoke?

Even in difficult and discouraging circumstances, the eye of the beholder can find beauty if it is truly desired.

The first area of your worship enrichment is in your basic approach to worship—your attitude toward it. We have already established a definition: *Worship is the expression of a relationship in which God the Father reveals Himself and His love in Christ, and by His Holy Spirit administers grace, to which we respond in faith, gratitude, and obedience.*

If we regard worship as the expression of a loving relationship between God and His people, then we will be prepared to accept our responsibility for our part in that expression, and we will see our part in its proper perspective. I propose that there are at least three fundamental attitudes that will make our worship more like what God intends it to be.

Worship As Dialogue

First is to understand worship as dialogue. I find this concept universally in those who think and write about worship. That is why I have placed it at the heart of our definition.

If we genuinely understand and believe that worship is dialogue, our approach to it will be seriously affected. It demands, for one thing, that we recognize the supremacy and power of God. If it is the Almighty God, the Ruler of the Universe, King of Kings, and Lord of Lords, before whom we gather ourselves, then I daresay we should not speak until we're spoken to. What are we to say, and how can a dialogue proceed, until we have been humble and wise enough to let God speak to us?

What do I mean by this? It is not that we go to church and hope that God will somehow reveal Himself in some unexpected or unusual way. Our joy is to know that He has spoken to us graciously in Christ (see Heb. 1:2) and that He welcomes, in fact, *seeks* for us to worship Him (see John 4:23). The reality of dialogue is potentially present in every kind of worship in our churches, but I doubt whether many Christians consciously and deliberately approach worship in that way. We might if we were stopped and asked about it, but my objective is to be sure that we do ask ourselves, and respond accordingly.

What an awe-inspiring and exciting thing it is to contemplate an encounter with Almighty God. That is why we so often turn to Isaiah 6 in describing worship. God is high and lifted up, seated on a throne in the temple; His glory, the mystery of the living creatures, the smoke, and the shaking foundations strike the prophet with awe and wonder. Something of that needs to be in our attitude toward our worship.

We already mentioned the beautiful figure of awe and wonder in the vision of Jacob (see Gen. 28:10–17). The ladder rested on the ground and its top was in heaven, and the angels went up and down on it. That magnificent traffic is a picture of the mutual ministries of the dialogue of worship. God declares His love and shares His grace, and we send up our prayers, our praise, our adoration and devotion.

It will not be difficult for you to visualize a heavenly dialogue in your own service of worship. Different portions of our worship are different parts of the dialogue. It is not rigid or stereotyped. A choir may be singing an anthem that is directed to God. It is their praise to God, in which we join spiritually. But it may well be that in that moment God, by His Spirit, directs a special word of grace to you, and the music that was "ascending" becomes grace "descending." In the same way, the sermon is certainly a word from God to us as worshipers. Yet mysteriously it may also be the worship offering of the preacher to God. We will shortly have occasion to look at the major parts of our worship services and identify their part in the dialogue.

Which part of the dialogue is of greater significance? That is not the proper question. The problem has always been one of balance. Some churches spend more energy on one side of the dialogue than on the other. It may be true that a given church feels that the gathering of the saints is for instruction from God and His Word through the sermon and that the response is in the life of the church outside the gathering. Yet that view denies to the gathered church its corporate work of appropriate praise, prayer, and obedience.

I am pleading for fullness in worship, a dialogue that is a rich and recognized conversation between God and His people. I'm not interested in counting how many angels go up the ladder versus how many come down. I do want the ladder busy.

Worship As Offering

A second basic attitude toward worship is in the understanding of worship from our human perspective as offering. There is a sense in which the teaching of our Lord is again confirmed in the experience of worship. It is more blessed to give than to receive.

I freely concede that we do not have anything to give to God until He first gives to us. We cannot love God without His first loving us; we cannot address Him without His first addressing us. Yet, once loved and once blessed, the way for us to receive is to give, and the proper way into the presence of God is with our offering.

Psalm 96:8 reads, "Ascribe to the LORD the glory due his name;/bring an offering, and come into his courts!" First Peter 2:5 describes the church as "a holy priesthood, to offer spiritual sacrifices acceptable to God through Jesus Christ." We should always approach our corporate worship with the question, What can I bring and offer to God in this service of worship that will be pleasing to Him?

Much of a worship service, other than the sermon, is for bringing our offering of spiritual (and material) sacrifices to God. Just as the preacher is filled with concern and eagerness to give properly in the name of Jesus Christ a message that will build up God's people, as worshipers we are to be filled with concern and eagerness to give properly our offerings to God. Peter wrote of us as a priesthood, not as individual priests, and in this instance it is because we need our brothers and sisters in order to make our offering what it should be.

Understanding that worship is an offering will close off to us, in many ways, the oft-repeated complaint, "We don't get anything out of the worship service." What if getting something out of it wasn't the point of the service? What if it was intended, rather, as an opportunity for us to bring something to it? If we are aware that worship is not for our enjoyment or approval, but for the glory of God, then we will utilize the vehicle of worship rather than evaluate our personal rewards. That is our first order of business as a worshiping congregation—to *give*. That is what love is all about, and to love God is to give God our obedience and adoration.

That principle does not act as an escape for poor leadership in worship. It is never fair to beat down the legitimate complaints of a frustrated congregation by mouthing pious phrases about giving instead of getting. If people are not "getting" something from worship, the question "Why not?" cannot be avoided. If they are not being taught in the principle of offering, then the leaders must accept some blame. If the people sincerely desire to bring their offering, but in various ways are frustrated or hindered in that desire, then once again the leaders must accept responsibility. Meaningful worship depends on each of us giving ourselves fully to the task. As a worshiper I am to be concerned about my offering. As a worship leader I am to be concerned both about how I instruct and how I make it possible for God's people to bring their offering.

The Old Testament "offerings" are helpful for our understanding of the principle of giving in worship. The worshiper brought what was his own, usually costly in relation to his resources. He identified himself with the offering, and in the case of animal sacrifice, the death of the offering was the release of life for the worshiper. We, too, should consider our worship to be the offering of our entire lives to God. Nothing will transform our worship experience more than our willingness to offer all as we participate in the divine dialogue.

Worship As Dynamic Growth

The third attitude that will be helpful in our quest for meaningful worship concerns the matter of respect. If we recognize that worship from our human standpoint is dialogue and is best expressed as offering, then we must also recognize that those expressions will be dynamic in their growth and as varied as the human family itself.

At this very moment there are believers in Christ gathered for worship in various places around the world. Some will silently stand as clergy in vestments walk solemnly to their place before the holy table. Some will sing and clap to the rhythm of drums, or dance their way around their meeting place in holy joy. Some will chant the Psalms, some will strum the guitar and make up the song as they go along. Which one of these does God not approve, or if He approves all, which one is best?

If worship is in Spirit and in truth, then perhaps the great disqualifier would be to claim that blessed Spirit for ourselves in a judgmental or restrictive way. When He came at Pentecost He entered in grace and joy into all—men, women, old, young. This would seem to be a mark of His continued work and presence—an openness to the variety of persons and cultures that so strikingly stamp the human family.

Jesus taught that we dare not come before God with our offering and have anything on our part that alienates us from our brother (see Matt. 5:23–24). That does not mean we tolerate everything that might be done in the name of worship, since the wisdom from above is first pure, then peaceable (see James 3:17). But it does mean that when we are truly before God, we should be conscious that we are there with all our brothers and sisters who also call upon His name in good conscience.

STUDY GUIDE

1. Read Genesis 28:10–17 and Isaiah 6:1–8. Reflect on the ways in which you have been conscious of worship as dialogue. When has God spoken most significantly to you recently? What has been a special part of your response?
2. How do the various parts of your service fit into the idea of dialogue?
3. What parts of your service enable you to make an offering?
4. How does the Old Testament offering help us understand what we do in worship?
5. Why is attitude so important for our worship?

14

Your Participation in Worship

Far too many people are satisfied with too little in their Christian lives. Many tend to measure experience in terms of quantity. Many good Christians confuse busyness with godliness, and far too many churches seem to feel that their calling is to provide some kind of church activity for every unclaimed moment in a parishioner's life. My interest is in making your experience of worship a constant source of gratitude to God and a source of growth because of its quality.

A practical way to enhance our worship experience is to examine our personal participation in worship and observe how it can be maximized. This is the point at which our individual commitment to Christ is expressed.

Preparation

Worship preparation is a constant process, but at some point it must become intentional. We may not think much about next Sunday on the preceding Monday, but why not at least by Saturday? As a preacher I am constantly aware that a Sunday at my best does not usually follow a Saturday at my worst. I have no brief with legalism at this point, but the late show on Saturday night does not make for vital worship the following morning.

Sunday morning is even more critical, and for some it is downright difficult. When my children were small it seemed to me that their minor disasters and difficulties were all reserved for enactment until Sunday morning. My wife was our music director, so any problems we had were compounded. I have every sympathy for people with high resolve and low performance in the matter of arriving at church in a state of spiritual and mental composure. But the intent must remain.

I heard recently of one parent who shares with his family at their Sunday breakfast the monetary offering that they will make and includes that as a part of their prayer at table. That is one creative way of helping to set your mind toward offering yourself in worship.

Preparation continues as we gather for worship. There is great variety in our churches, even in how we come together before the service. In some places there is a subdued and quiet atmosphere, a minimum of conversation. Often that is possible because of the physical environment. In other churches there is a great deal of conversation, recognition of friends, casual remarks, and very little opportunity for reflection or quiet meditation.

Neither of those extremes is all good or all bad. It is a pleasant problem if people are so friendly they have to pay attention to each other. If there are not spacious areas outside the church, or weather is inclement, visiting by Christian friends at their first encounter might be expected. Nor is quiet an automatic indication of spiritual maturity or careful worship preparation. I might suggest that part of the problem is deciding when the service begins. There are some necessary noise and distraction just in the process of getting a sizable number of people into their places. If a congregation feels that silence is the appropriate environment for worship preparation, then I would suggest that the pastor and any others involved in leadership join the congregation at that time. The standard for pre-service conduct should be agreed upon and reasonable.

Worshipers who want to prepare for worship in a private and individual way might include in their preparation a careful review of the order of service, a reading of any indicated Scripture or hymns, and prayer for themselves and their fellow-worshipers.

Some churches have decided to put the announcements and similar matters of church interest at the very beginning of the service and in this way put them "outside" the worship. Others have decided that such matters are part of the common life of the body of Christ and are not "unworthy," but should be properly included in worship. Nearly all of us would urge worship leaders to train congregations to read their bulletins and to force church organizations to use means other than worship service announcements to inform their constituents.

Preparation for worship in many Reformed churches includes a confession of sin and a declaration of pardon. If we refer to Isaiah's experience in God's presence (see Is. 6), we can understand the response to the divine presence as a deep awareness of our unworthiness. This has not been universally practiced as a specific liturgical action, however, though it has, of course, been a part of prayer. Penitence is appropriate for the Christian who comes into the presence of God.

Since public confessions are most often generalized prayers, an individual sense of release from guilt that might be expected is seldom experienced. Thus, Lutheran churches have a direct absolution. The pastor declares the sin forgiven. But whether there is pastoral declaration or not, the Christian can pray for forgiveness with biblical assurance that God truly forgives us in Christ (see 1 John 1:9). If there is a prayer of confession in your liturgy, don't just say it, *pray* it, and rejoice in God's forgiveness. If not, lift your heart to God in penitence before the service and prepare yourself for the exciting work of worship.

Some churches have very little in the service that could be called preparation. It is probably assumed that corporate worship just "picks up" on a life of fellowship with

God that includes penitence, praise, and prayer. If that is the case, then the individual must be sure that preparation has indeed taken place. Worship is bound to be more meaningful if there is deliberate preparation for it.

Praise: Adoring God and Giving Thanks

When I talk about praise, I am including the twin virtues of adoration and thanksgiving. There is a proper theological distinction between the two.

Adoration is the joyful and awesome contemplation of God. It is the reminder of the excellency of His glory and the magnificence of His works. It is the recounting of His mighty acts of creation and redemption, and the humble acknowledgment that He is God and there is no other. Jesus Christ reflected His adoration of God in the first statement of the Lord's Prayer, "Hallowed be thy name" (see Matt. 6:9; Luke 11:2).

It is obviously a very short step from adoration to thanksgiving. When we recall the goodness, greatness, and grace of God, the natural response is gratitude.

Put this all together and we are talking about praise. That is the root meaning of *Hallelujah*, or *Alleluia*, a universal exclamation of praise. Most of us settle for singing it rather than saying it. That does enable us to be together in it, but it is still the same cry of praise.

Personal Participation

I want to emphasize again our need of conscious and intense participation in worship. The psalmist calls for our praise again and again. "Let everything that breathes praise the LORD!" (Ps. 150:6), and "all that is within me, bless his holy name!" (Ps. 103:1).

Some of us will find more opportunity in our worship tradition for praise than others. I don't think the key is necessarily quantity, but it certainly is quality. Use what is there in your particular liturgy. Perhaps you do little more than sing the doxology, but it is a profound ascription of praise. I have often observed a congregation listlessly singing these great sentiments of praise to God from whom all blessings flow. We even call on the heavenly host to join in our anthem. If I were part of that heavenly choir, I might fire back the suggestion that we get into it a bit more before calling on outside aid.

Praise is never something that awaits circumstance or emotion. It is always right to praise God, and it is always a good thing. That is why our corporate worship is such a healthy activity. Thus the ancient prayer, "It is fitting and right to sing to you, to praise you, to worship you in every place of your dominion." It calls on us to join our fellows in the praise of God, regardless of our present condition. Such deliberate praise of God will do much more to bring wholeness to your spirit and joy to your soul than waiting for a surge of joy and then voicing your response to God.

If we are worship leaders, we must ask if we are giving adequate opportunity for people to participate in corporate praise, thus leading them into a deepening experience of personal praise. When we seek to give glory to God, it is a transforming process. We become like the One whom we adore.

Music

When we looked at Methodism and Lutheranism, we noted the increased use of hymns in public worship. To this day, evangelical Christians have a friendly awareness of the way hymns and other music help us offer praise to God. In many Protestant churches, the hymns are the single overt expression of the people in worship. They deserve our careful attention.

Let us look first at the relationship between music and

text. Music is a God-given avenue of expression from the deepest and most complex recesses of our inner selves. It is essentially emotional, even though there are aspects of the structure of music that might appeal to our minds. Music moves us by combinations of sounds and rhythms to which most of us are amazingly susceptible. We quickly develop firm musical tastes. And although we know what we like, we seldom know why. We also sense when the text—the words—seems to fit the music, each interpreting and enhancing the other. There is no question that music increases the power of the words, which already have a significance of their own. For one thing, music enables us to memorize the words easily. We will remember a song long after we would have forgotten the words by themselves.

The majesty of hymnody, then, is the combination of meaningful content and emotion. We can repeat songs without being bored by the repetition, which is more than we can say for most sermons! Music holds an awesome power for shaping our lives as Christians, and that power should be exercised in a responsible way.

The staple of church music is the hymn, a song of praise to God. The use of hymns dates from Bible times. As we have seen, some groups in the church have confined their singing to settings of Scriptures, while others have also sung the poetry of gifted authors.

Perhaps the greatest shortcoming in the use of hymnody is our failure to take the text seriously. As a result, we do not pay attention to what is being said in the hymn, or we select music not appropriate for the particular moment in worship.

Another form of church music is the gospel song, which can loosely be distinguished from the hymn in that it is addressed to the congregation rather than to God. Having said this, however, it is fair to note that the Psalms flow rather freely between talking to God and talking about God. One thinks of Psalm 23: "He restores my soul. . . . thou art with me; thy rod and thy staff, they comfort me." A hymn or song becomes a proper part of worship not because we all know the tune and like to sing it, but because it moves forward our particular act of worship.

As participating worshipers, we must enter into singing to the fullest extent possible to express our praise to God. Become familiar with your hymnal. The various indexes in the back are useful, especially for finding different tunes for familiar words (metrical index), or a number of hymns by the same composer or author. The mysterious names of hymn-tunes come from various sources, including places associated with the tunes or the composer (e.g., "Duke Street," and many of the Welsh tunes). The numbers often printed in the headings (8.7.8.7.D) are the number of syllables in each line. CM is Common Meter (8.6.8.6), LM is Long Meter (8.8.8.8), and SM is Short Meter (6.6.8.6). Many churches settle too quickly for a rather thin serving of hymns when the possibilities are enormous.

But in addition to hymns and songs there is the music that is sung or played for us. Here the average worshiper is called upon to accept what is provided. My concern is for us to approach music in worship so as to benefit most from it. There is an assortment of choral, solo, and instrumental music for our worship services.

Choir music originally confined itself to service music, that is, sung portions of the liturgy. This was done to assist the congregation in responses (antiphons) or chants that might be difficult. Then more and more the choir took over portions of the service, especially in the cathedrals. In most of our churches today, a choir is not thought of as assisting a congregation as much as it is performing for the benefit of a congregation.

If we remember our model of dialogue as the basic form

of worship, then the choir should either be acting as a vehicle for God's Word to the congregation or expressing something to God on behalf of the congregation. If we regard it that way, we will be open to an anthem's message to us, or we will identify ourselves with its praise to God. In either instance the performance aspect is always secondary. I do not regard the "performance" as meaningless or unimportant. If the choir is addressing us with God's Word, that expression deserves the same excellence that we expect in a sermon. If the choir addresses God on our behalf, our offering should be as worthy, as beautiful as we can make it.

I presume the same criteria apply to solo or small group singing in worship. It can take either side in the dialogue, and as a worshiper I should relate to it as such. I think the problem comes in the way in which the artist serves the dialogue.

Our culture is filled with professional performance, which combines aesthetic beauty and personal accomplishment. I find no problem with this. On television or in the concert hall we hear capable artists who diligently prepare, and we enjoy the music and appreciate the skill of the performer. For us it is the pleasure of an experience of excitement and beauty. For the performer it is the thrill of performance, the applause, the reward. It is apparent how different that is from worship, where the ultimate concern is the glory of God.

How tragic, then, if the church becomes a concert hall and the worshipers, any of them, become performers. A Greek Orthodox priest whom I know attended a well-known evangelical church and complimented the preaching. But he characterized the rest of the service as a "Christian Lawrence Welk show."

I really have no objections to people gathering to hear someone sing, or a choir sing, and responding with delighted applause. I just don't want to call that worship. I would also observe that since worship is dialogue, the involvement of the congregation is such a precious and proper thing that everything else must serve that involvement.

I have not mentioned instrumental music. For a long time, I failed to see the possibility of offering something to God through the playing of instruments, even though the Bible speaks so clearly of this. I was so word-oriented that I regarded instruments as valuable only for accompanying the singing of a sacred text. But one must consider that the instrument is the "voice" of a worshiper and that in that moment I can rejoice in, and in a sense join with, the offering of the instrumentalist.

That understanding also affects the question of playing music that has no recognizable text associated with it. The music as offering has its own validity. It is not made pleasing to God because it has sacred words. It might be more pleasing to me, but that is not the final criterion of its meaning if it is an offering to God. I will also quickly admit that the musician wants me to hear it, too, and he or she therefore has an obligation not to offend unnecessarily. But I am trying to enable us as worshipers to find in music a vehicle of praise. Once we see it in those terms it will open us to rich experience.

Those principles are of great importance for worship leaders, and are far too often ignored. It is no particular help to the church, for instance, that "gospel" is now a type of entertainment music along with rock, country and western, and other styles.

Prayer

All worship includes prayer. We have seen the various traditions, with prayers written and prescribed, with prayers suggested and modeled, and with prayers extemporaneous. What will assist us as worshipers, regardless of tradition, in this spiritual exercise?

Certainly we understand that prayer in worship is corporate, so it is *our* prayer—the prayer of a corporate priesthood—that is being raised to God. Perhaps that is obvious to some, but I have found many Christians who seemed to think corporate prayer was a time for everyone to pray their own prayers as best they could. It is our privilege to pray with the person who leads us and respond to the prayer with a sincere *Amen*, "so be it." Most of us say Amen in our hearts, but Roman Catholics, Lutherans, Episcopalians, many Pentecostals, and most black churches will say Amen aloud. The latter groups will say Amen all during the prayers as well, and perhaps that was what led many Protestant groups to drop the custom.

The audible Amen has a long tradition both in Judaism and Christianity. In 1 Corinthians 14:16 and 2 Corinthians 1:20, Paul made clear that an audible Amen by the congregation was normal. That would only continue a well-established practice in the synagogues of that day, and one that has remained to the present. I can find no good reason why it should not be a part of our liturgy today.

A major Protestant development has been the pastoral prayer, or "long prayer." This is still a practice in many churches and I presume some congregations find it helpful. However, the tendency for effectiveness in such matters is for briefer segments. That does not mean that less time totally would be given to prayer, but it would be in shorter sequences. A pastoral practice that seems effective is to divide the pastoral prayer into discrete parts. The first section may be used for thanksgiving, the second for intercession (relating to matters outside the congregation), and the third for petition (congregational needs). This benefits from a good theological structure in placing our own concerns last. How we pray both reflects and instructs our theology.

My prejudice is that prayer for a congregation should be prepared. In some traditions a written prayer would seem to open to question the genuine godliness of the leader. I have observed that usually such churches will not look down on "sermon notes," and they are blessed in the singing of written hymns. Perhaps they would not look down on "prayer notes."

As a pastor I am impressed that leading a congregation in prayer is a significant and responsible act. I know we can pray anytime and anywhere, but the importance of prayer for a congregation should not be limited by my own mental restrictions. I am well aware that God is gracious and hears us, not because we say it well, but because we come by faith through Christ. But remember, we are talking about finding the fullest possible potential for our worship experience. For many of us, this would include the privilege to pray the same prayers that saints like John Chrysostom, Francis of Assisi, or Luther prayed.

For traditions in which prayers are set, it can be hoped that opportunities for silence will increase so that personal intercessions can be made. I have also observed quite often a lack of vision and resourcefulness on the part of liturgical worship leaders. Mission concerns are often neglected, and I find virtually no church leaders praying regularly for fellow Christians and other churches in their own community. To hear our prayers, you would assume that we were the "only show in town."

All of us lament our lack of prayer. Do not be afraid to enter into the time-tested prayers of our ancestors in the faith, and above all, let corporate prayers be your own prayers in the deepest sense possible.

Scripture Reading

Every worship tradition makes a place for the public

reading of Scripture. We have seen how this came into the church from the synagogue, and from the very beginning Christians have heard read and expounded first the Old Testament, then the "memoirs of the apostles," as the Gospels were called in the ancient church, and finally the completed New Testament. The maximum number of readings has been three: Old Testament, Epistle, and Gospel. It should be noted that the Psalms were used as responses to the readings or as hymns, not as the reading itself.

The practice of Scripture reading as part of worship has varied in Protestant churches. As sermons got longer, often Scripture reading got shorter. Today many churches that are quite committed to the Bible will still have very little Scripture reading in the service. Much of the time it will be the text for preaching, possibly read as the beginning of the sermon.

There is undoubtedly some thought behind this practice. Certainly Scripture reading was more valued when there were no Bibles available. Perhaps some pastors reason that people are reading their Bibles at home. In many churches the members will participate in Bible study classes as well as at times of worship. Yet none of these is really sufficient to make public Scripture reading unnecessary. I suspect that it is also observed that the listeners don't always "get that much out of it." Part of this is due to poor reading. Some Scripture lessons are given no preparation and little interpretation in context with the rest of the service, and it is no wonder that they are not well received.

Part of our problem is in not being able to read together. The vast number of translations (many more than are needed, I fear) makes for unwanted variety. Many churches are resorting to pew Bibles, or at least to printing out the lessons so that the congregation can read together.

Whatever may be the practice, your worship experience has a potential for enrichment in hearing the Word of God.

Historically, virtually all churches stood for the reading of the Gospel to indicate the reverence paid to the Word about Christ. First Timothy 4:13 advises, ". . . attend to the public reading of scripture, to preaching, to teaching." That is the suggestion to a church leader to give proper place to the reading of God's Word. We should do the same, and we should listen expecting to hear something that will bless us and build our faith.

Scripture reading is one place where we can use lay participation to great advantage. I know of a Lutheran church that often assigns readings to a family, with several participating. Preparation and even rehearsal, however, are important, and church leaders often don't want to take the time to coach those who are to read. I'm afraid that some just don't want to relinquish the pulpit, even for that short activity. The problem is really one of style. If the approach is casual and things are done on the spur of the moment, it is much easier to do it yourself than to involve those who are less experienced.

We have already mentioned that some churches use a lectionary, or list of readings for each Sunday. It is an easy matter for a church to use one of the many available (Catholic, Orthodox, Lutheran, for example) or to make its own. Following the Church Year can be an exciting experience in worship, and it does serve to guarantee that all the major themes of the faith will be covered each year. More and more, it appears that evangelical churches are rediscovering and using the Church Calendar.

Preaching

What a wide range of style and content we find in our pulpits! Part of my task is the study and teaching of preaching, and I am astonished at the great variety presented by contemporary preachers. There is an astounding number of good preachers today, and the most meaningful and productive contact between a pastor and the people is still the sermon. There are relatively few churches that prosper with a weak pulpit. The change in the inner cities has meant that churches that were famous as preaching centers fifty years ago are now in eclipse. The populations are suburban, and there are thousands of very good churches that have no reason to become well known outside of their own community, but that are blessed with constructive programs and excellent preaching.

Preaching is also a part of the divine dialogue, and for this reason both the Holy Spirit and the congregation play a large part in the effectiveness and stature of its preacher. If a church wants a good preacher, then it will protect the means by which good preaching comes; time for reading and study, maximal lay leadership in organizational and functional matters, freedom from innumerable committees, extra time on leave for study, and support for preaching by prayer and enthusiastic feedback are all important elements. Whatever gifts any preacher may have will expand unbelievably if they are challenged and supported.

Approach the preaching with a spirit of expectation and openness, and I mean this whether you are clergy or laity. Churches with more formal liturgy must create space for the proclamation of the Word. Since Vatican II, the Sunday Mass in Roman Catholic churches is always to include a sermon. Our task is to ensure the excellence of Christian worship, and that especially includes the sermon.

Our earlier discussion of sacraments and symbols implied the great importance of the Word of God. It is no mistake to speak of Word and sacrament together, since the sacraments could never come into existence without the Word. That does not detract from the significance of sacraments, but it keeps the Word in its proper place: indispensable.

Preaching in the church is the continued presence of Christ with His people, giving His instruction by the power of the Holy Spirit. In fact, in the church it is Christ who preaches. The reaction of some people to that statement could well be a dropped jaw of disbelief. "You haven't heard our preacher!"

Speaking as a preacher myself, my own jaw drops with you. By what stretch of the imagination could my stumbling and inadequate words, or even my smooth and adequate ones, be considered the preaching of Christ?

Let me remind you that this is part of the offense of Christ and of the gospel. It has to do with the miracle of the Incarnation. The same amazement comes to us when we contemplate the idea of how God could become fully and completely resident in humanity. Full divine nature takes on full human nature in Jesus Christ. And we believe and adore.

I will admit there seems to be *more* required in the way of faith when we ask for preaching by us who are sinners to be the Word of God. I am profoundly impressed when I take a long look at what I have said and what I now say. There is so much I do not wish to blame on God. But the miracle remains that when the Scriptures are faithfully proclaimed, God by His Spirit accomplishes His work in our hearts. He does this in and through the folly of preaching—stumbles and all.

Preaching in behalf of Christ does not require that I must judge the divine authenticity of every sentence. Yet neither can I claim immunity from examination through the principles and precepts of the Word of God. Jesus said concerning us preachers, "He who hears you hears me" (Luke 10:16). And Paul reminded the Thessalonians that "when you received the word of God which you heard from us, you accepted it not as the word of men but as what it really is, the word of God, which is at work in you believers" (1 Thess. 2:13).

In one sense, it is our word that becomes the Word of God in preaching. But in another sense the Word of God is Jesus Christ Himself and the revelation of Him who by the Holy Spirit is preached to us and through us. Honestly, if I did not believe that when I get up to preach God will speak, I would not do it! So it is not my word. But I do say it, and God graciously allows Himself, indeed He desires, to be present in that event.

Do you see what this can do for your worship? Can you dare to believe that you meet with your fellow Christians to *hear from God*? And if you really believe that, can you regard it as a pleasant option, or just a Christian duty, rather than a great privilege? I'll admit that this does make boredom the cardinal sin of Christian preaching. Imagine being bored by the Word of God!

Do you think Moses had trouble staying awake on Sinai? Did Elijah yawn generously in the cave while watching the fire and earthquake? Yet in how many places is the sermon the cue for wool-gathering, counting the panes in the windows, thumbing through the hymnbook—anything to "get through" the next several minutes. I have every sympathy with the problem, for I have had it myself many times. But remember, we are exploring the way to make worship—your worship—its very best. You can't change the preacher, but you can pray for that person and be a part of the process that creates good preaching. And you can expect and look for God to speak to you in the sermon.

I might add parenthetically that encouraging honest feedback can do great things for a preacher. I have heard the pious statements from preachers to those who reported they "enjoyed" a sermon. One usually protests that "sermons are not be be enjoyed," or, "Don't thank me, thank the Lord." I find this a bit amusing. Think of the discouragement if the response was, "I did not enjoy that sermon. I'm sorry I came," or even worse, stony silence.

Jesus knew that at least half the battle in speaking is the listener. "He who has ears, let him hear," He said (Matt. 13:9). What a treasure would be yours if every time you heard a sermon you would carry away at least one idea that blessed and enriched you.

The sermon is one of the two major parts of worship—intercessory prayer being the other—that is genuinely contemporary. If a Christian from a thousand years ago could visit your church he would recognize and understand a great deal. He might not know the tunes, but he would understand the words. He would especially perk up if it were a baptismal service or a Eucharist. But the sermon would need explaining. The text might be familiar, but the life situations, the issues, the reference points, would be strange—and they should be. Preaching in its best understanding is bringing the Word of God from first century Jerusalem or earlier right into the twentieth, and to the place where you live. Some preachers don't work hard enough on that, but to bring God's Word to the present is the point of preaching.

Giving

The offering in most of our churches is vastly underrated as a part of our worship dialogue. Some suggest that from the human side of the interchange, no moment is more significant than the presentation of our gifts to God.

Our best approach to worship is in terms of offering. If we are conscious of our Christian stewardship, we present our gifts to God first of all, and then to the church, His ministry in the world. Our offering of money becomes extremely significant. It is a good thing to give praise to God, to sing, to pray, to respond to spiritual instruction. Such worship is not without effort, energy, and devotion: it is *work* (remember, *liturgy* means "the work of the people").

Somehow the depth of that devotion is reflected in our generosity with our money. The Scriptures teach both tithing and proportionate giving. The Bible also makes it clear that God has a claim on all that we do not give away. It matters, then, how we spend our money. In no sense does token giving please the Lord, nor a casual approach to our offering as though the amount is meaningless.

The amount of my gifts tells you nothing, and Jesus warned that I should not publicize it. But the amount of my gift tells me something about myself and my heart for God, and it is certainly noticed by Him. David said, "I will not offer burnt offerings to the LORD my God which cost me nothing" (2 Sam. 24:24). Paul said, "God loves a cheerful giver" (2 Cor. 9:7).

The presentation of the offering should be a joyous occasion when, with brothers and sisters in Christ, I have opportunity to present my gifts to God. It is a glorious action, and I am convinced that it is not properly celebrated in our churches.

Perhaps we feel apologetic about speaking of money. But an offering that is being made to God is another matter altogether. In this act of worship, it is not a question of reaching the budget or supporting a cause. We are giving because we need to give, and we are offering those gifts to God as part of our sacrifice of praise and thanksgiving. That is such a grand and joyous act it should never be sublimated for fear of offending someone who doesn't understand what is being done. Worship is the privilege of gathered Christians, and our giving to God should indeed be "cheerful."

Make the most of this event regardless of the custom of your church. Some congregations receive offerings that are taken up and then sort of disappear while the service continues. There's nothing terribly wrong about that, but I do feel it deprives us of an important moment that helps express our devotion to God. I know of one large church where the people stand just as the ushers pass them in procession to the front of the church. It forms a kind of wave of people standing, identifying themselves with the offering being brought, and then joining in the doxology. But you as a worshiper, regardless of the liturgical action of the church, can prepare your gift. Then with a joyful heart present it to God, and truly worship Him.

Preparation, praise, prayer, Scripture reading, preaching, giving—that list covers almost everything that happens in your worship service. The potential for blessing, for meaning, for participation in the dialogue is exciting. If you can understand your role of full participation in the drama of worship, then the psalmist will not seem so odd when he says, "I was glad when they said to me, 'Let us go into the house of the LORD!' " (Ps. 122:1 NKJV).

STUDY GUIDE

1. What has been your experience of "preparation" for worship? Is the congregation a help or hindrance? The leaders? When do you think the worship service begins?
2. What place does music have for you in worship? What do you consider to be the purpose of a choir anthem? a solo? an instrumental number? Examine the use of hymns in several of your recent services.
3. What is your usual attitude toward prayer and Scripture reading in worship?

4. Six different events in worship were discussed. In which do you feel you excel? What needs help?
5. What do you feel you can do to help produce good preaching in your church? Can you accept the idea that preaching is the Word of God?

15

Worship as a Way of Life

You will remember that when we looked at the Roman Catholic sacramental system, we discovered an attempt to provide a means of grace that would extend to people's lives from the cradle to the grave. The Protestant church rejected some of that theological definition, but it did not reject the underlying principle. That principle is the blessed reality of a worshiping community indwelt by the Holy Spirit, and responding together in obedience and faith to every significant moment of our lives.

We may speak in jest about going to church when you're hatched, matched, and dispatched, but that does not destroy the reality of the place of the worshiping community at all the high points of life. Let us look at those major events with an eye to their place in our worship experience. How does the worship of the church become the shared experience of the entire spectrum of our Christian lives? We will discover that virtually every Christian tradition feels the necessity of a congregational and a liturgical response to the mountain peaks of our lives.

1. Initiation: Baptism, Dedication, and Confirmation

Regardless of our tradition, we all recognize the significance of the two stages in our lives of birth and our passage into adult responsibility. Baptism is our Christian "rite of initiation" that speaks to this entire sequence. Christians who live in families all know that the event of welcoming a child demands a communal response. So we meet as a church and carry out our theological tradition.

If we baptize infants, we acknowledge that salvation, as a gift of God through the work of Christ, is freely given apart from anything that we can do, and that the children of believing parents do properly share in all the blessings of Christ's redemption. The parents answer for the child and promise to provide the guidance and influence that will bring this child to a full expression of faith at the time of maturity.

Where infants are baptized, the church knows that initiation into Christ is just that, and that something else remains to happen. That will be "confirmation," a confirming of baptismal faith, an actualizing of what has been potential. In recent times, confirmation has taken on the form of an academic graduation, and faith has become equated with the right answers to some theological questions. Most church leaders recognize the problems in this process, and serious attempts are being made to press for commitment to Christ in confirmation. Also, the need is seen to make confirmation late enough in life to insure that the decision is mature. It is disappointing to discover that the profession of a preteen often withers with the demanding issues that face the late adolescent.

If our tradition makes baptism available only to the believing, confessing person, then we still feel deeply the need to respond corporately to the birth of a child. So we have a service of dedication, and we commit believing parents to the same responsibilities for Christian nurture as in infant baptism. We would then await the child's own commitment to a personal, meaningful faith, at which time we would administer baptism.

In both traditions, salvation is understood as a gift solely dependent on God's grace through Christ, not to be received through any human action. At the same time, we recognize the need for each person's conscious and public affirmation of his or her personal faith and identification with the body of Christ. The problem for children who have been nurtured in Christian homes and churches is, when is the appropriate time to expect a confession of faith as the genuine response of the mature person? Just as confirmation has sometimes been misused, some groups baptize rather young children whose later years throw serious questions on their childhood faith.

Both groups of Christians are dealing with the same set of problems and solving them only partially. Initiation embraces the whole process of birth and growth, and we must remember that it is an initiation into the body of Christ and the Christian community, not just a sociological process of maturing. Most theologians and church leaders have become sensitive to the need for meaningful commitment at all points of worship action. Parents are answering serious questions. Candidates must be properly instructed and examined. All of us as worshipers are involved as well, receiving people into our fellowship, committing our support and loving care.

Initiation in any of its phases takes place within the worshiping community. You and I, as part of Christ's church, are deeply involved in every baptism, dedication, or confirmation. We are not bystanders, we participate in this rite. We are also reminded of our own initiation, and the promises and meanings of it. In some churches, there are now specific services for the renewal of baptismal vows. All of this is healthy motion toward meaningful worship.

2. Eucharist

If baptism is the sacrament of initiation, Eucharist is the sacrament of nurture. If we are born anew into the body of Christ, then we need to be fed and to grow. This is only one of the profound meanings of the Eucharist, but it does explain why it is properly oft-repeated. It is not the only means of nourishment for the Christian, but it gathers together in one act all the things that nurture us. Above all, it speaks eloquently to the fact that our life is dependent completely on the Lord Jesus Christ.

We have already looked at historical and theological matters relating to the Eucharist. In every tradition, there does seem to be a deepening sense in our day of the importance of the Lord's Supper. We can pray, and continue talking together, that the Lord's Table will be a true expression of the underlying unity of faith and life among Christians, rather than something that illustrates our separation from one another. The consistent prerequisite for coming to communion is that we be repentant toward God and have love for our neighbors. Unfortunately, reconciliation and unity are defined pretty much on our own individual terms. According to Paul and early Christian teaching, however, the bread was a symbol of the unity that is the body of Christ, many grains made into a single loaf.

All of us struggle with ways to make the Eucharist what the name implies—*a thanksgiving*. We are the inheritors of a service that has as its primary focus a penitential quality to it. We seem more concerned about our sins and their forgiveness than about the thanks we can give to God for our creation, preservation, and redemption.

The Eucharist is the remembrance of the entire reality of Christ's incarnation—His life, death, resurrection, ascension, and return. It is the anticipation of the great messianic banquet yet to come, and it is the celebration of Christ present with us to give strength and joy for our journey. This is where you can make your worship a constant experience of offering yourself in love to Christ and of receiving Him in your heart by faith. The mystery of bread and wine being taken, eaten, and then transformed into our very selves is an eloquent parable of Christ indwelling us and making us one with Him as He lives in us.

Jesus Himself requested that we do this in remembrance of Him. Nothing should be more genuinely welcomed than our opportunity to fulfill His express wish, thus remembering Him by participating in His life. Just what does this "remembrance" imply?

In this age of science fiction we are used to "time-machine" stories that project a person forward or backward. What if we were given the opportunity to be transported to Jerusalem in the first century and be with Jesus and the disciples in the Upper Room, to follow the bloody path to Calvary, and then to visit the empty tomb? Would you take that offer, or decide it was not all that attractive? All of us as Christians maintain that we were indeed there, that what was happening to Jesus embraced our history. Would any of us say no when asked, "Were you there when they crucified my Lord?"

This is what the remembering (Greek, *anamnēsis*) is all about. The quality of such an experience is wide open to you: you are in Christ; you were there. Regardless of your particular tradition, you can be one of the grateful communicants who finds your heart burning within you, just as the two who walked with Jesus on the Emmaus road and saw Him "in the breaking of the bread" (Luke 24:35).

3. Reconciliation

Early in the history of the church came the sacrament of penance, the ministering of the grace of forgiveness by a priest to a confessing, contrite Christian. This was necessarily tied to what is known as auricular confession—the verbal confession by the offender to the priest in private, and the requiring of certain acts of contrition to demonstrate the genuineness of one's repentance. That practice has fallen on hard times, even in the Roman Catholic church since Vatican II, and is being replaced or supplemented by a service of reconciliation, a small group activity with a more general confession and absolution (forgiveness).

Few Protestant churches have practiced anything that comes close to auricular confession. The need for repentance and forgiveness of particular offenses is left a private matter, and corporate confession remains rather general. Is that enough for the community to do in worship?

That there is a need for the unburdening of guilt and for a sense of forgiveness and release cannot be denied. In many instances the psychiatrist, psychologist, or counselor has taken the place of the priest to hear confession and pronounce forgiveness. Yet, according to James, the church is to be a community where one can "confess your sins to one another, and pray for one another, that you may be healed" (James 5:16). How this is to be recovered in our churches remains to be seen. The development of small groups in many churches has moved us more in the direction of openness and trust. What we do together in worship symbolizes that relationship and goes a long way in providing the climate for a deep level of sharing.

4. Healing

The ancient church also had a sacrament of "extreme unction," which was anointing with oil and praying for a person who was thought to be dying. The arrival of a priest in those circumstances often made the person worse rather than better. But, like confession, the roots of healing are found in Scripture. The modern history of the healing ministry for the sick in Catholic, Orthodox, and Protestant churches has been a patchwork of widely diverse actions. There have been both flagrant abuses and stubborn denials of healing that are embarrassing, and there have been very quiet movements that are deeply spiritual in their impact.

A Christian response to illness that includes the church at worship is common. All our traditions include prayers for the sick. Some traditions have included more than this. The early church certainly practiced anointing sick people with oil, which included a laying on of hands in prayer. The oil was often drunk as well as applied. Such action had certain medical significance in ancient times. It would be more symbolic today. But do not forget our discussion of the power of symbols and the earlier openness of the church to God's actions through such vehicles.

Today we must take seriously the reality of sickness as both physical and spiritual. That is not to say all sickness is a result of sin or demonic power. It is to say that our bodies are profoundly affected by our minds and souls, and the spiritual aspect should be part of our treatment. That, by the way, is behind the principles of today's holistic medicine.

I am not debating whether people are healed by the power of God through faith and prayer. There are too many instances of healing that do not follow the normal processes of recovery, and we can only be grateful for such events. The point for us is broader than that. Illness is a very significant event in our earthly pilgrimage, and there should be something in our common life as Christians that recognizes and in faith responds to it.

Many churches today have services of special prayer for the sick. These are found in all worship traditions. Many groups practice anointing and laying on of hands, and knowledgeable people in medicine are not critical. There are comfort and strength in the awareness that the community has responded to our personal crisis and we have felt the touch of love for healing. The careful use of this approach can mean nothing but good in the church. We should shun exploitation or the raising of false hopes, but we should minister positively and fearlessly in the name of Christ.

5. Weddings and Funerals

What important events are weddings and funerals in our lives! They are also important events in the life of the Christian community, although there has been in the past a tendency to remove them from the environment of worship. A funeral was never defined as a sacrament because there is no visible sign of an invisible grace. Yet we all can see the need of response by the Christian community to the death of a member. That response becomes instructive regarding our own death, and it fills a very real need for the bereaved family.

Historically, the day a Christian died came to be referred to as his or her "eternal birthday." This explains why you will find in older books on the lives of saints an entry after the name that looks like this: † 462. Neither the date of birth nor baptism appears; this is the coronation date, the day the person finished the race. The funeral, therefore, is a proper sendoff of the saint to the church enrolled in heaven.

The Bible is strangely silent regarding any normative practices for weddings and funerals. But tradition surrounding them is very powerful, and we are seeing anew the need to review constantly what we do in those significant moments. Some observations apply to all traditions.

The church is the proper environment for both services. Wedding chapels and funeral homes may do for those who are not living in a community of faith, but normally not for the Christian.

If the services are set in the context of worship, then this should determine some of the activity. In the early church, weddings took place in Sunday worship, just before the Eucharist. Much of today's practice is properly outlined in the service books of various denominations, but we all need to view these ceremonies as calling for our participation. Prayers, congregational songs, responses—things that have gradually left these ceremonies—need to be heard again.

6. Other Rites

Ordination

This service of corporate worship is important to the life and health of the church and is therefore assumed to be important to the members of the worship community. It is naturally quite significant to the clergy. Ordination not only says something about the calling and gifts of the ones ordained, it also says something about the ministry of the church. Every Christian is called and set apart to serve Christ in the world; some are officially set apart to serve Him in the church. Baptism marks that "ordination" of all Christians to be Christ's new people, in service for all humanity.

Those "ordained" by prayer, laying on of hands, and other ceremony are recognized by the church as gifted in ways that will enable the church to perform its ministry under the lordship of Christ by the power of the Spirit. They are servants of the servants of Christ. Historically, ordination was a sacrament called "orders," as it still is in the greater part of Christendom.

The church does not "ordain" everyone to his or her particular task. An electrician can certainly be led of God and glorify God in his work. But he is not as such "called" by the Spirit and given gifts and abilities in electricity so that the church could obey the Word of God and do God's work in the world. We are all to serve God and our neighbors by what we pursue as a vocation. The ordained are "church-directed" in their vocation.

Each of us as a worshiper may take part in the communal responsibility of qualifying the servants of the church for their tasks.

Private Worship

An important part of our Christian life is our worship of God in private, or in circumstances other than the gathered congregation.

It has been assumed from the very beginning of Christianity that worship would be the constant, daily expression of the Christian's devotion. The basic component of this is always prayer. The models are deep in Old Testament faith. Prayer was made by Israelite priests at the time of morning and evening sacrifice (see Ex. 29:38–39). Psalm 55:17 mentions prayer three times a day, and Daniel followed that pattern (see Dan. 6:10).

That threefold action commended itself to early Christians. In addition to New Testament references, there are references to such practice in the *Didache*, Tertullian, Origen, Cyprian, and others.

Certain historical events profoundly affected the direction of this devotional pattern. If you will read Acts 10, you will note that God gave specific directions to both Cornelius (while not yet a Christian) and to the apostle Peter as they prayed at specified hours—Cornelius at the ninth hour (3:00 P.M.), and Peter at the sixth hour (noon).

The major event surrounding devotional patterns in the postapostolic era was the rise of monasticism. Those were essentially communities of prayer, and the development of a rigorous schedule of prayer was inevitable. Psalm 119:164 says, "Seven times a day I praise thee," so that became the model. One more prayer was added to those seven, which were eventually called the Divine Office and appropriately designated as follows: Matins or Nocturns, the small hours of morning; Lauds, daybreak; Prime (first hour), early morning; Terce (third), midmorning; Sext (sixth), noon; None (ninth), midafternoon; Vespers, sunset; and Compline, bedtime. These were also known in the New Testament and later as the Hours, and there were many different ways of reading, praying, singing, and meditating that were prescribed by different monastic orders.

Though present today in Roman Catholic and Orthodox practice, that system of devotion did not move readily into Protestantism. Cranmer did establish morning and evening prayer in the Anglican church, and Luther also made provision for Matins and Vespers. These were presumably services of worship to be held in the church, but they were also recommended as forms for worship at home. Certainly many Christians privately read daily the Scripture lessons, psalms, and prayers that were provided.

The vitality and the theology of most of Protestantism, however, was away from all that smacked of "Romish formalism," and the challenge to the individual Christian was to chart his own course of private piety. This was marvelously aided by the new availability of the Bible because of the printing press, and this opened to the reader the possibility of personal reflection on Scripture along with prayer—really, of course, the core of monastic devotion as well. If you read the Divine Office you would read all of the Psalms once a week and the rest of the Bible in large portions. But in most Protestant communions the procedure for private worship was optional.

In Protestantism, the many spiritual awakenings, the call for personal conversion, the vigorous pulpit ministry, and the increased involvement of laypersons in various aspects of church ministry all served to increase the commitment to personal devotional life. Along with this came numerous printed devotional plans and publications. Almost every denomination has a devotional guide for daily prayer and Bible reading.

We previously observed that congregational vitality in worship is of necessity tied to the level of worship commitment away from the gathered church. There is a sense in which the church at worship is giving thanks for the blessings and presence of God that it has seen and known in its daily life. If we return to our concern for worship as offering, then we will certainly be bringing to God the praise and petition that have been generated in the life of faith day by day. So we are saying that corporate worship is just that much richer if it arises from an experience of daily, intentional encounter with God.

Let me offer two suggestions with regard to personal worship. First, try to be disciplined without being legalistic. Don't set impossible goals and don't add to your sense of guilt when you fail. Some of us have experienced a pietism that was certain that if you did not have a quiet time early in the morning the day could not go right. Conversely, prayer time equals a good day. That easily becomes a kind of vending machine piety. Put the prayer in the slot and out will come a happy day.

Yet would any of us say that prayer will *not* make a day better? Of course not. Days may not be all that good with prayer, but we pray nonetheless. Private worship is like corporate worship. It is not a means to an end. It is not to pile up points on some spiritual score card, but to set apart both the day ahead, and yourself, for the Lord's use. It has its own unique reward.

Second, get all the help you can through the mutual encouragement of fellow Christians. Most of the time our private prayer is much too private. When we are not accountable to anyone, we have a strong tendency to lapse. The home, husband, or wife, may provide that accountability, but not always.

We may have access to a small group of friends in a Bible

study or fellowship group. Our church may have some challenge for commitment to daily reading and prayer. But do not overlook the help from friends that can encourage us and keep us honest. Most Christians who have persevered in private devotions have developed habits, a time and place that become a part of their normal life. Family devotions, usually at table, are a help, although small children will force a certain relaxation, openness, and brevity to the occasion. A sense of humor will also come in handy.

I do not want you to minimize the healthy effect of meaningful corporate worship on our private devotional life. The order, regularity, and discipline of the gathered church that are always the expressions of our combined piety help to overcome our individual weakness and unfaithfulness. That is why regular worship is so important. It will constantly infuse the sense of the presence of Christ into the daily affairs of our lives. For the Christian, the week begins on Sunday and the direction and tone of life are set again and again by our service of worship.

Worship—Our Life in Christ

You have suspected by this time that worship is probably far more inclusive a term than might first be thought. You are right.

Our classic text for this truth is Romans 12:1: "I appeal to you therefore, brethren, by the mercies of God, to present your bodies as a living sacrifice, holy and acceptable to God, which is your spiritual worship." The King James Version translated it, "reasonable service." It is the word we looked at in the very first chapter, *latreia*, which means "service," but that special kind of service that is directed toward God. We serve God by "presenting our bodies as a living sacrifice." This is the "body language," if you will, of worship. We are taking our very selves and making them the response, our offering to God.

Just as Jesus gave Himself, we give ourselves. The cross was not the only moment of Jesus' self-giving, it was the ultimate moment. He gave Himself in every breath, thought, and action of His whole life. We are to do the same. We live our lives through and in our bodies, and if we give our bodies to God we are giving all.

We can only present our "life" in little bits. We experience life as a stream of moments which we have, only to lose in the darkness of the past. The continuing reality is our body, and in the constant presentation of it we properly worship God. We do this symbolically when we gather for worship. We present ourselves, in concert with our brothers and sisters, to confess our allegiance, to open ourselves to divine inspection and communication, and to receive the assurances of grace and love.

But we go from the service of corporate worship into the service of individual worship, never away from the presence of God, never to be called to anything less than the incarnation of His love and the vehicle of His will.

STUDY GUIDE

1. What significant events in the life of your family can you identify with a service of worship?
2. What are the problems that are presented to the church when we baptize infants and when we don't?
3. How does your experience affirm or deny the communion service as a Thanksgiving (Eucharist)?
4. How do you feel about the practice of anointing with oil or of the laying on of hands for those who are sick?
5. There is an increase in the number of burials or crema-

tions without a service. What is your opinion of the value of a funeral?

6. Why should a congregation be involved in a wedding ceremony?

7. What are the devotional aids suggested by your church? What is the relationship between private and corporate worship?

16

Before We Say Amen!

Let me gather up the different threads of our exploration and see what is before us in this grand adventure of worship.

As I survey the experience of most Christians in worship in our churches I believe there is one major problem area. Perhaps *problem* is the wrong word, because the matter does seem to carry a certain occupational hazard, which is built into worship and has been present from the very beginning.

I refer to the task of keeping in balance the potential forces in corporate worship so that our *adoration and praise* of God are worthy and our *nurture and reception* of grace and strength are adequate. There is an amazing duality that is present in our worship, and though I do not think any of us are perfect worshipers or meet in perfect churches, perhaps the awareness of that duality will keep us open to growing experiences and move us toward such perfection.

We saw the duality in worship first in the Old Testament struggle between *priestly* and *prophetic* movements. The New Testament and early church witnessed the developing tension between the *structured* and the *spontaneous*. This can easily be expanded into a debate between *liturgy* and *liberty*, which is probably an expression of the choice between the *subjective* and the *objective*. I was nearly through college before I understood those last terms, so let me elaborate on them.

Subjective and Objective Worship

Subjective worship is concerned with what happens to worshipers—how they are edified, moved to deeper commitment, impressed by the Spirit and the Word with the love and grace of God. I have often been struck with the dominance of this understanding of corporate worship when I have been in prayer with church leaders prior to a worship service. We pray for the preacher, that the Word would come with power and effectiveness. We pray for the people, that they would receive just what they need that day, and especially for any who are not Christians, that the Word would be received in faith in their hearts. Prayer for the choir and for the worship leaders follows the same vein, so that everyone would receive the strength and help required for his or her pilgrimage. I say Amen.

Objective worship is concerned with what we do toward God in our service. It is concerned with our side of the dialogue, and it concentrates on the words and acts that would convey to God and to each other the sincerest feelings and resolves of our very selves. Prayer before a service in this mold would be for all of us that we would make an acceptable sacrifice of praise and thanksgiving and that God would be glorified by what we say and do. No worship should be without both its subjective and objective sides, its push for *impression* and *expression*. The problem is balance.

The tension here underlies the question of the place of Word and sacrament in worship. And it certainly is the deciding factor in the question of the place of *mind* and *body* in worship. An illustration of this for me is the discussion that might arise regarding a kind of worship with the body, liturgical dancing. Some of us would find this an impossibility for our worship service. Some might barely tolerate it if it were adequately explained and tied securely to sacred text and music. Some of us would accept it, if done well, just as we would an anthem or a solo. Whether or not we like liturgical dancing is not the issue. We are showing how the understanding of what worship is all about will lean in one or the other of two directions, both important.

I believe that if we will set our minds to worship God objectively, subjective worship will be present. But if our goal is to pursue the subjective, to "try to get a blessing," we are likely to jump the track on objective worship. It's the lesson of Christ: if we seek first the Kingdom of God (here, objective worship), all these things (subjective worship) will be added unto us.

Evangelism and Nurture

Not exactly the same, but another duality is the matter of evangelism and nurture. Some churches are the scene of constant appeal for commitment to Christ as the focus of corporate worship. Other churches seem never to consider the possibility that someone in attendance might be outside the Christian community. This may be partly a theological question, but the polarization is often present and needs to be examined carefully.

How evident that the worship of the church should be full and rich in its range and scope! I am not ready to believe that everything is fine as long as some group somewhere is doing the various things we have seen to be properly a part of worship. It is not just the idea that if you like spontaneity you can go to this church, and if you like structure in worship you can go to that church.

Such thinking is the result of the mistaken idea that there is a God-given right to "worship as we please." The God-given right is to worship, but our Christian responsibility (and privilege) is to worship as God pleases. I cannot but feel that His will for His children is a fullness of grace—an abundant life—and I am deeply impressed that this embraces the spectrum of worship reality.

During the 1970s numerous churches experimented with different types of services. The early service might be the "family" service with more informality, a different set of songs, and a lot of spontaneity. A later service would be traditional, more formal, with less congregational participation. There are some commendable qualities of such a procedure as long as there are consistent attempts to expose the two "congregations" to each other and to the kinds of worship expressions that characterize them. Such education is necessarily slow and sometimes a bit painful, but it is the way to growth.

I am not thereby convinced that there is "one way" to worship. But I am convinced that careful observation of our worship practices in light of the rich traditions of the church may well open up new vistas of blessing and meaning that were previously closed to us.

There are other problems facing the church as a worshiping community. The pressure to get everything within a weekly one hour is devastating. There is no way that the proper ministry of the church in worship, education, outreach, and many other areas can be accomplished in one hour a week. On the other hand, churches that meet more often and longer must look carefully at the purpose of such meetings.

It may not be that two "worship" services each Sunday are needed. I always feel that if the church is at worship, everyone should come. Worship is "for God," and that should never be optional. But it is not fair to call a time of fellowship, or a musical, or a lecture, "worship." Such gatherings are perfectly fine and meet needs, but worship is more than meeting needs. It is meeting God.

To Be with Him

What are the prospects for worship? For you they are magnificent. You are privileged to engage in the finest, grandest expression of all the creatures of the universe—the worship of God. It is the occupation of the angels and the ultimate purpose of all things, whether living or inanimate.

The same God who is praised by the silent beauty of a hundred billion galaxies is pleased to receive your adoration and worship. Jesus told us that the Father seeks for those who will worship in spirit and in truth. I can do what a galaxy cannot. I can participate consciously and deliberately in the worship of the Father, Son, and Holy Spirit. How awe-inspiring it is for me to realize that worship was and is the gracious work of Christ the Son. I am in Christ, I am part of His body, and therefore in the Spirit I participate in the adoration and obedience He always gives the Father.

What greater joy can there be for the follower of Jesus than to be where He is? We have seen the glorious promise of His presence where two or three are gathered in His name. There has to be something about that presence that is more, or at least different, than when I am alone. Jesus is always with us, but His presence is promised in a special sense when we are "gathered" to be with Him. He has told us that in eating bread and drinking wine we are to remember Him and that this remembrance is a sharing in His body and blood (see 1 Cor. 10:16). Can anything be more significant for the follower of Jesus than to be in His presence? I think not.

The prospect is for you to determine to maintain a heart of worship. The tradition of which you are a part, or of which you will become a part, makes possible in its worship a glorious dialogue. You can engage in it.

You can bring your offering and join the company of heaven in the praise of God. You can hear the voice of God and draw aside to see a bush that burns with fire and is not consumed. You will take the shoes off your feet, only to put them on again in order to walk the paths of obedience and service.

And you will continue the rehearsal in preparation for joining what the seer of Patmos envisioned (Rev. 5:13-14): "And I heard every creature in heaven and on earth and under the earth and in the sea, and all therein, saying, 'To him who sits upon the throne and to the Lamb be blessing and honor and glory and might for ever and ever!' And the four living creatures said, 'Amen!' "

Amen.